LATTER DAY SAINT BELIEFS

A Comparison Between the RLDS Church and the LDS Church

Steven L. Shields

Herald Publishing House
Independence, Missouri

Library of Congress Cataloging in Publication Data

Shields, Steven L.
  Latter Day Saint Beliefs.
  1. Reorganized Church of Jesus Christ of Latter Day Saints—Doctrines. 2. Church of Jesus Christ of Latter-Day Saints—Doctrines. 3. Mormon Church—Doctrines. I. Title.
  BX8675.S54   1986   230'.9333   85-27300
  ISBN 0-8309-0437-9

Printed in the United States of America

89 88 87   86   3   4   5   6

CONTENTS

INTRODUCTION

Ever since the death of Joseph Smith, Jr., in 1844 rival factions of the Latter Day Saint movement have been vying with each other for recognition as the legitimate successor to the original church. In the past, the rivalry between the two largest organizations—the RLDS church,[1] headquartered in Independence, Missouri, and the LDS church,[2] headquartered in Salt Lake City, Utah—has often been contentious, with one side making accusations about the beliefs of the other which may or may not have been accurate.

Because of the larger numbers and wider recognition of the LDS church, the RLDS church has felt a need to identify itself as a church that is "not the one in Utah." This identity crisis was primarily the basis for most of the literature aimed at pointing out the differences between the two churches.

Fortunately, in more recent times, the relations between the two churches have become more amicable. Each church has its own distinct identity. Each church has its own program. Each has its own conception of mission. Historians and other scholars from each organization are actively involved in the joint research and study of the history of the Latter Day Saint movement and its doctrinal development.

At this point in the relationship between the two church organizations perhaps there is a need for a renewed effort on the part of the RLDS church to present differences between itself and the LDS church in a more positive light. Undoubtedly the age-old question will continue to be asked of RLDS church members: "What is the difference...?" So our responsibility is to let the facts speak for themselves—to state RLDS beliefs and let them be compared with LDS beliefs with no argument as to why one is "right" and the other "wrong." Serious investigators, who approach decisions such as this in the right spirit, will discern the best answers for their individual situations.

I have written this book with general readership in mind, although realizing that a majority of the readers will have some background in the Latter Day Saint movement. As a seventy in the RLDS church, and a former member and missionary of the LDS church, I am reasonably well-versed in the doctrines and teachings of both organizations.

It has not been possible to go into great detail, nor to cover every single point of difference between the two churches. However, I have been careful to present each church's beliefs fairly and sensitively. I have used extensive references to support ideas, and to allow the beliefs of each side to be presented. The LDS church position is supported by quotations from LDS church leaders, whose writings and authority have either been stated directly by the church, or have gained widespread acceptance in the church, ascertained by the sales and numerous reprintings of their writings. Even so, members of the LDS church express different interpretations of church belief in different parts of the world. While LDS readers might take issue with some facet of doctrine presented herein, they should understand that my purpose has not been to discredit their beliefs.

My sincere hope is that this volume will assist honest investigators to understand more about the Latter Day Saint churches, that it will continue to foster the increasingly friendly relations between members of both organizations, and that RLDS church members will find in this work sound information with which they can better represent the church to their friends.

Steven L. Shields

---

1. Reorganized Church of Jesus Christ of Latter Day Saints.
2. Church of Jesus Christ of Latter-day Saints.

1

GOD, JESUS CHRIST, AND THE HOLY SPIRIT

The nature of God and the composition of the God-head is perhaps one of the most significant areas of difference between the RLDS church and LDS church. One reason for this wide difference in interpretation is possibly because Joseph Smith, Jr., after having witnessed a vision of God and Christ, was unable to relate exactly what he saw. From the time of his "first vision" until his death he left no less than nine different accounts of this one event.

Another reason lies in the different understandings between the two churches on the position of the prophet and the manner in which the prophet's teachings become scripture or doctrine for the church.

It is readily apparent to the student of the scriptures that an absolute description of an infinite being is impossible. And, as can be ascertained by the many recorded testimonies of those who have experienced him, God seems to mean something different from one person to the next.

In the well-known account of Joseph Smith, Jr.'s first vision, he relates that on retiring to the woods to pray about which church to join, he was visited by God the Father and his Son Jesus Christ. Appearing to Joseph in glory and power, described as being brighter than the noonday sun, they told him not to join any church. This first event in the Restoration movement is significant for Latter Day Saint believers because it laid the foundation upon which Joseph later built.

A basic tenet of the early church, as written by Joseph Smith, Jr., and published in 1842, states: We believe in God the Eternal Father, and in his Son Jesus Christ, and in the Holy Ghost. While the LDS church has retained this verbatim as the "first article of faith," the RLDS church has opted for a broader interpretation.

In 1970, the Basic Beliefs Committee of the RLDS church published a volume expanding on this brief statement:

We believe in God the eternal Father, source and center of all love and life and truth, who is almighty, infinite, and unchanging, in whom and through whom all things exist and have their being.

We believe in Jesus Christ, the Only Begotten Son of God, who is from everlasting to everlasting; through whom all things were made; who is God in the flesh, being incarnate by the Holy Spirit for man's salvation; who was crucified, died, and rose again; who is mediator between God and man, and the judge of both the living and the dead; whose dominion has no end.

We believe in the Holy Spirit, the living presence of the Father and the Son, who in power, intelligence, and love works in the minds and hearts of men to free them from sin, uniting them with God as his sons, and with each other as brethren. The Spirit bears record of the Father and of the Son, which Father, Son, and Holy Ghost are one God.[1]

Although the RLDS church affirms that God is unchangeable and eternal, our understanding grows and takes on new meaning as we progress in our knowledge of the gospel and receive continuing revelation through the Spirit.

The Basic Beliefs Committee explained some of these difficulties in attempting to describe God:

From the very outset we encounter a formidable difficulty in expressing ourselves with respect to the God in whom we believe. As soon as we endeavor to make some affirmations about reality which go behind the world of immediate experience we recognize that we are limited to the language and symbols of finite experience. We are endeavoring to employ words from a human context to describe what is more than human. Clearly we are driven to the language of analogy and parable, and must bear in mind that our accounts are at the same time partly literal and partly nonliteral. Thus we describe God as "Alpha and Omega," as "jealous," "angry," as "well pleased," as "infinite," and try to remember that such terms say something about God that is meaningful but can by no means say everything about him that is true.[2]

The position of the RLDS church is that God is personal. We refer to God as "our Father" because our relationship with him is not unlike that of a child and a parent. This is not to imply that the RLDS church believes God has physical form like a human, but that there are personal attributes found in our experiences with God such as freedom, truth, creativity, love, and beauty.[3]

Jesus Christ is at the very center of the RLDS faith. He has approached us on our ground, by becoming mortal and living among humankind for a period of time. That he lived and taught and died for our sins is an accepted fact of Christian history. Because Jesus Christ is God, or, if you prefer, a part of the Godhead, we begin to understand something more about the nature of God. We see in Christ the love of God, love that was plainly evident in Christ's personal ministry.

We believe that Christ was the one through whom the world and its inhabitants were created. This affirmation is borne out in the ancient scriptures as well as modern:

And by the word of my power have I created them, which is mine Only Begotten...and worlds without number have I created, and I also created them for mine own purposes; and by the Son I created them.[4]

Possibly the most important aspect of Christ's ministry on earth was his sacrifice for all humankind, and his resurrection. This is the underlying theme of the entire New Testament canon of scripture. The authors of *Exploring the Faith* explain how important this is to RLDS believers:

The Cross takes on meaning only in the light of the One who hangs upon it, and no talk of Resurrection has meaning which does not focus upon the Person who was resurrected. It is not some general principle of human survival after death that is being preached.... It is a story written, like the parable of the prodigal son, which carries no impact for those who have not come to know Jesus and the power of life he taught and embodied.

Jesus' rising from the dead brought the assurance that no work of sin or bond of death could restrain the power of life which men had encountered in him.[5]

Other RLDS authors have gone on to state the following:

The church testifies to the fact that Christ continues to live and act in the world and that the world is a new place because of his victory over death.... Our proclamation of Jesus Christ is meaningful because we believe that he is our Savior.

Jesus Christ is the central figure in the faith of the church. We proclaim that the resurrected Christ is the Lord of the universe and that he gives us the gift of salvation. He is the key to our understanding of God and of ourselves.[6]

While Christ was ministering in Palestine, he taught his disciples that another comforter would come and take his place after he had gone. These early believers had difficulty in understanding this at first. The great day of Pentecost in the early church marked the turning point in their comprehension of the eternal principles of the gospel.

We have today the testimonies of the early church to guide us, and also our own experiences with the Holy Spirit which help us to understand more about

God. Indeed, as Joseph Smith, Jr., stated, "The glory of God is intelligence, or in other words, light and truth."[7] In that same section, he previously had said, "Truth is knowledge of things as they are, and as they were, and as they are to come."

Through the Holy Spirit God is revealed to us; God's will for the church is revealed to the prophet.

We experience God not only as the Father, but also as Jesus Christ and the Holy Spirit. Our affirmations about God also apply to Jesus Christ and the Holy Spirit. Although our understanding is that there is but one God in these three, we make a distinction between them. Jesus Christ as the Son of God refers to the historical Jesus of Nazareth, but also to the living Christ who is experienced in our lives. The Holy Spirit is the power and presence of God in the lives of many people of all ages. The Holy Spirit can work in all those who open their hearts and minds to the power of God.

* * *

The LDS church theology of God has undergone change since the early declarations by Joseph Smith, Jr.

When the LDS church became established in Utah, Brigham Young taught the following:

> When our father Adam came into the Garden of Eden, he came into it with a celestial body, and brought Eve, one of his wives, with him. He helped to make and organize this world. He is Michael, the Archangel, the Ancient of Days! about whom holy men have written and spoken—he is our father and our God, and the only God with whom we have to do.[8]

A number of other LDS church leaders during the same period also taught the same thing. This "theory," as present-day leaders call it, has been denounced by them as a false doctrine.[9]

While the purposes of God might be understood similarly by the RLDS and LDS churches, the LDS church teaches that God is a resurrected man—that he once lived on another world and earned godhood by obeying the gospel.

Attributing this teaching to Joseph Smith, Jr., the LDS church quotes him thus:

> God himself was once as we are now, and is an exalted man, and sits enthroned in yonder heavens!...I am going to tell you how God came to be God. We have imagined and supposed that God was God from all eternity. I will refute that idea, and take away the veil, so that you may see....It is the first principle of the gospel to know for a certainty the character of God, and to know that we may converse with him as one man converses with another, and that he was once a man like us; yea, that God himself, the Father of us all, dwelt on an earth, the same as Jesus Christ himself did; and I will show it from the Bible....

> Here, then, is eternal life—to know the only wise and true God; and you have got to learn how to be gods yourselves, and to be kings and priests to God, the same as all gods have done before you, namely, by going from one small degree to another, and from a small capacity to a great one; from grace to grace, from exaltation to exaltation, until you attain to the resurrection of the dead, and are able to dwell in everlasting burnings, and to sit in glory, as do those who sit in glory, as do those who sit enthroned in everlasting power....[Such persons are] heirs of God and joint-heirs with Jesus Christ. What is it? To inherit the same power, the same glory and the same exaltation, until you arrive at the station of a god, and ascend the throne of eternal power, the same as those who have gone before.[10]

Whether Joseph Smith actually said this was debated between the two churches for decades. The problem arises in that the discourse from which the above quote was taken was not published until after Joseph Smith's death, thereby raising questions for the RLDS church as to its authenticity. In addition, RLDS church members find it difficult to support this idea from the scriptures. (A separate chapter will discuss the differing views of revelation and the position of the prophets in presenting church doctrines.)

The LDS church, then, teaches that there are other worlds with other gods, that God was once a man as we are, and that all men can become gods over their own worlds.

Believing that all men are literally spiritual offspring of God, the LDS church teaches that there is also a "Mother in Heaven." The church, in a formal pronouncement by the First Presidency, stated:

Man, as a spirit, was begotten and born of heavenly parents, and reared to maturity in the eternal mansions of the Father.... all men and women are in the similitude of the universal Father and Mother and are literally the sons and daughters of Deity.[11]

Jesus Christ, as the Son of God, is considered to be the mediator between God and human beings, that he seeks to turn humankind from sin to righteousness, and strives to lead all persons to perfection in order that all might live with God after the resurrection.

It is believed by the LDS church that "mortal persons who overcome all things and gain an ultimate exaltation will live eternally in the family unit and have spirit children, thus becoming Eternal Fathers and Eternal Mothers."[12]

In an official publication, the LDS church beliefs about Christ are stated thus:

Christ is our Redeemer and our Savior. Except for him there would be no salvation and no redemption. Unless men come unto him and accept him as their Savior, they cannot have eternal life in his presence. The gospel plan is the way that is ordained whereby men may come to him and find salvation....

Salvation by grace is a glorious doctrine of Christ. Although confusion and false teachings relative to it are found on every hand, the same is true with reference to the Godhead and almost every other principle of salvation.

Grace is simply the mercy, the love, and the condescension God has for his children, as a result of which he has ordained the plan of salvation so that they may have power to progress and become like him....

Christians speak often of the blood of Christ and its cleansing power. Much that is believed and taught on this subject, however, is such utter nonsense and so palpably false that to believe it is to lose one's salvation. For instance, many believe or pretend to believe that if we confess Christ with our lips and avow that we accept him as our personal Savior, we are thereby saved. They say that his blood, without any other act than mere belief, makes us clean....

Salvation in the kingdom of God is available because of the atoning blood of Christ. But it is received only on condition of faith, repentance, baptism, and enduring to the end by keeping the commandments of God.[13]

(The different perspectives on salvation as understood by the two churches will be discussed in a separate chapter.)

The Holy Spirit, or Holy Ghost as the LDS church generally states, is explained by a prominent church authority:

The third member of the Godhead. He is a Personage of Spirit, a Spirit Person, a Spirit Man, a Spirit Entity. He can be in only one place at one time, and he does not and cannot transform himself into any other form or image than that of the Man whom he is, though his power and influence can be manifest at one and the same time through all immensity...he is the Comforter, Testator, Revelator, Sanctifier, Holy Spirit, Holy Spirit of Promise, Spirit of Truth, Spirit of the Lord, and Messenger of the Father and the Son, and his companionship is the greatest gift that mortal man can enjoy.[14]

After new members have been baptized into the church, both the RLDS and LDS churches perform an ordinance called "confirmation" wherein the right to receive the Holy Ghost or Holy Spirit is bestowed by priesthood authorities.

The significance of this ordinance, on which both churches would generally agree, has been explained by Clifford A. Cole, former president of the RLDS Council of Twelve:

[The gift of the Holy Spirit] is God's response to the candidate's commitments in which the Holy Spirit enters into that life to strengthen, comfort, enlighten, teach, and guide the person in fulfilling the commitment. It is the promise of God to be one's constant companion if that person will continue to yield to the highest understandings of God's will.[15]

SUMMARY

1. The nature of the Godhead is a significant area of difference between the RLDS and LDS churches.

2. Basic to the Restoration churches is Joseph Smith's affirmation of a "first" vision, in which he reported seeing heavenly beings.

3. Both churches believe in God, the Eternal Father, his Son Jesus Christ, and the Holy Spirit.

4. The RLDS church believes that God, the Father, is a person without implying limitations of any sort. Jesus Christ is a person possessing the attributes of both God and humans at the same time. The Holy Spirit is a person, who is the living presence of the Father and the Son.

5. In RLDS belief, church members are free to increase their understanding of the Godhead as the Spirit reveals it to them. God is not to be restricted by definition.

6. Jesus Christ is at the center of the RLDS faith.

7. LDS theology on this topic has undergone change over the years. At one time the teaching was that Adam was actually God, the Eternal Father. This

theory, propounded by Brigham Young, has been refuted by modern church leaders.

8. The LDS church teaches that God is a resurrected man, and that all men may someday become gods over their own creations.

9. In LDS teachings, the Holy Ghost, or Holy Spirit, is a personage of spirit, and functions as the third member of the Godhead.

10. After new members are baptized, both churches perform an ordinance of confirmation wherein the new member is blessed with the right to have the Holy Spirit as a constant guide.

NOTES

1. Basic Beliefs Committee, *Exploring the Faith* (Independence, Missouri: Herald Publishing House, 1970), 10.
2. Ibid., 19–20.
3. Peter A. Judd and A. Bruce Lindgren, *An Introduction to the Saints Church* (Independence, Missouri, 1976), 34–35.
4. RLDS Doctrine and Covenants 22:21 b, c; LDS Pearl of Great Price, Writings of Moses 1:32–33.
5. *Exploring the Faith*, 45.
6. Judd and Lindgren, 51, 52, 54.
7. RLDS Doctrine and Covenants 90:6a; LDS Doctrine and Covenants 93.
8. *Journal of Discources*, Vol. 1 (Liverpool, England: F. D. Richards—with the approval of the LDS Church, 1855), 50.
9. *Deseret News 1985 Church Almanac* (Salt Lake City: *Deseret News*, 1984), October 9, 1976.
10. Bruce R. McConkie, *Mormon Doctrine* (Salt Lake City: Bookcraft, Inc., 1966), 321.
11. James R. Clark, *Messages of the First Presidency*, Vol. 4 (Salt Lake City: Bookcraft, Inc., 1970), 199–206.
12. McConkie, 517.
13. *What the Mormons Think of Christ* (Salt Lake City: The Church of Jesus Christ of Latter-day Saints, 1982), 16–18.
14. McConkie, 359.
15. Clifford A. Cole, comp., *The Priesthood Manual* (Independence, Missouri: Herald Publishing House, 1985), 228.

2

REVELATION AND SCRIPTURE

One of the most important doctrines for both the RLDS church and LDS church is that the canon of scripture is not full—that God continues to direct the church through revelation to the prophet. The practical application of this concept makes the Latter Day Saint churches unique among religions. There is also a clear distinction of practice among Latter Day Saint churches. Each one approaches this idea differently.

Over the years, the RLDS church has developed a concept of revelation that has progressed from understanding it as plenary, or propositional, to viewing revelation as conceptual, or an encounter with God which requires an interpretation by the recipient.

RLDS church leader Duane E. Couey defined this concept of plenary, or propositional, revelation as an understanding

that by some supernatural influence it is possible for prophets, apostles, or sacred writers to fully communicate truth without error. For this to be tenable, one would have to assume that it is possible for man to be completely drawn out of his finitude. That is, that within such an encounter he would really not be existent in his humanity at all, and then when the encounter was over he would strangely fall back to his finite and sinful state.[1]

This viewpoint has caused considerable difficulty as scholars have examined and studied the scriptures and historical development of the documents of the revelations presented to the church. One writer has observed that

one of the most troublesome complexities is evident when

looking at the Doctrine and Covenants. Here is found the experience of God's guidance so expressed as to indicate that the guidance is direct and propositional. The first person language, the indications of the prophet being directed to write, the content of the documents (often informational), all give the impression that revelation is an experience in which God gives persons direct answers to specific questions.[2]

In examining the various documents, church scholars have found that there have been numerous changes in the wording of many of the early revelations brought to the church. Joseph Smith, Jr., the founding prophet of the Latter Day Saint movement, made extensive modification to several revelations, some of which had been previously published.

RLDS church members have come to realize that interpretation is an important factor in understanding revelation and attempting to relate it to our current situation. This realization helps us to understand how Joseph Smith was able to modify the documents.

Richard Howard suggests that because of Joseph's sensitivity to both the events of history and the "continued striving of the Spirit of God" he was motivated to reinterpret his understanding of the principles and procedures that were most appropriate for the church. Such modification may indicate that, far from being infallible, the prophet is required to interpret the will of God in light of his own understanding, an understanding that grows and changes. Modification may also be necessary because the revelatory experience is one in which the prophet is challenged to intepret the will of God for the contemporary situation, not for all time.[3]

Because of these difficulties and the necessity for interpretation, as is evident in writings of the prophets of the RLDS church, a growing theory is that revelation is an encounter with God, in which concepts are presented through a higher level of communication. As has been observed, one of the most striking features of this alternative concept of revelation is a denial of the equating of revelation with revealed doctrines. Arthur Oakman has stated that it has been his experience that "revelation is actually always more than our apprehension or record of it." He notes that while there are "truths of revelation, there are no divinely communicated doctrines as such." There may be propositions which are the result of correct thinking about revelation, but these propositions are "neither that revelation nor directly revealed...."

In the theory of revelation as encounter, revelation is found as the basis of life. Revelation grounds new life; it calls people forward to service, hope, and meaningfulness.[4]

One of the primary functions of the prophet in the RLDS church is to speak forth for God to the church, and from time to time present documents in which the will of God is expressed. Although individuals and local church leaders may receive personal enlightenment to guide them in their daily affairs or administrative work, only the prophet is able to present revelations to and for the entire church.

But church members still recognize that the prophet is a human being—that ordination does not remove fallibility. Before a document is accepted as God's will it is presented to the church by the prophet for the sustaining vote of the membership in a delegate World Conference. This is in harmony with the principle of "common consent" requiring that "all things shall be done by common consent in the church, by much prayer and faith."[5]

This procedure of confirmation provides a system of checks and balances to ensure that the document is indeed of divine origin. RLDS church leaders and members have long recognized that because humans are fallible, they can be subject to temptation, pressure from society, or other influences. This should not be construed as a form of mistrust of the prophet, or other church leaders. In addition, it is not, as some might believe, a procedure whereby church members can pick and choose which doctrines to believe. Even though a prophet might present a totally new concept, it will still be supported by previously revealed scriptures. This process allows the Holy Spirit to work with individuals; it allows the true spirit of free agency and common consent, as established in God's law, to operate so that all have an opportunity to share in the revelatory experience.

Only when a document has been confirmed by the church membership can it be added to the canon of scripture.

Some church writers have observed that

as a church we have accepted certain unwritten criteria by which we recognize writings as scripture and as authoritative in our personal and corporate lives. These criteria include, but may not be limited to, the following: First, the tradition of the church. For example, we accept the Bible as scripture because Christians before us have accepted it as such for centuries. Second, scripture is given by designated persons. With very few exceptions, we accept as scripture, in addition to the Bible, only those documents that are presented to the church by its presidents in their capacity as "prophet, seer, and revelator." This is largely tradition and not a necessary requirement, however. Third, we check for continuity with other scripture. We accept into the canon of scripture only those writings which give supportive witness that builds upon those already accepted. A fourth criterion relates to what can be described as the "canon within the canon." Individual persons tend to select for their use passages of scripture which they find especially meaningful for their own lives.[6]

* * *

The LDS church takes a decidedly more conservative view of revelation and scripture. The process of revelation has been described as a method where the Lord appears personally to certain spiritually receptive persons; he speaks audibly by his own voice, on occasions, to those whose ears are attuned to the divine wave length; the angels are sent from his presence to minister to deserving individuals; dreams and visions come from him to the faithful; he often speaks by the still small voice, the voice of the Spirit, the voice of prophecy and revelation; he reveals truth by means of the Urim and Thummim; and he gives his mind and will to receptive mortals in whatever ways seem appropriate as circumstances require.[7]

As with the RLDS church, only the prophet in the LDS church may present revelations for the entire church. Various church leaders and individuals may receive personal revelation to guide them in their lives and administrative responsibilities.

Although the LDS church does not regularly add documents to their scriptures as is done in the RLDS church, they readily affirm that revelation takes place and is essential to the operation and claims of the church. A prominent LDS church leader has written the following:

Since The Church of Jesus Christ of Latter-day Saints is the Lord's true Church; and since the Lord's Church must be guided by continuous revelation if it is to maintain divine approval; and since we have the unqualified promise that this Church and kingdom is destined to remain on earth and prepare a people for the Second Coming—we could safely conclude (if we had no other evidence) that the church today is guided by revelation (Doctrines of Salvation, vol. 1, pp. 279–283). It is true that not many revelations containing doctrinal principles are now being written, because all we are as yet capable and worthy to receive has already been written. But the Spirit is giving direct and daily revelation to the presiding Brethren in the administration of the affairs of the church.[8]

The role of the prophet in the LDS church is of such great importance, and is accorded such high respect, that members of the church have created a situation where the prophet "is not infallible, but he would never lead the church astray." This idea can be clearly seen by the following:

Revelations given of God through his prophets, however, are not subject to an approving or sustaining vote of the people in order to establish their validity. Members of the church may vote to publish a particular revelation along with the other scriptures, or the people may bind themselves by covenant to follow the instructions found in the revealed word. But there is no provision for members of the Church to pass upon the validity of revelations themselves by a vote of the Church; there is nothing permitting the Church to choose which of the revelations will be binding upon it, either by a vote of the people or by other means. Revelation is revelation. When the Lord speaks, he has spoken. His word is to be accepted and obeyed if men expect to receive salvation. To reject the word of the Lord is to reject the Lord himself to that extent.[9]

The late LDS church president Spencer W. Kimball has elaborated on this idea:

Every normal person may have a sure way of knowing what is right and what is wrong. He may learn the gospel and receive the Holy Spirit which will always guide him as to right and wrong. In addition to this, he has the leaders of the Lord's church. And the only sure, safe way is to follow that leadership—follow the Holy Spirit within you and follow the prophets, dead and living.

No one in this Church will ever go far astray who ties himself securely to the authorities whom the Lord has placed in his Church. This Church will never go astray; the Quorum of the Twelve will never lead you into bypaths; it never has and never will. There could be individuals who would falter; there will never be a majority of the Council of Twelve on the wrong side at any time. The Lord has chosen them; he has given them specific responsibilities. And those people who stand close to them will be safe.[10]

Scriptures

Several books are accorded scripture status by the RLDS church and the LDS church. These scriptures are the standards by which doctrine and church government are formulated. Each of the two churches publishes its own editions; therefore, some differences have evolved over the years which require explanation.

Both churches use the Bible. The RLDS church uses what is known as the Inspired Version. This is an edition of the Bible, based on the King James Version, which was corrected by Joseph Smith, Jr., through the spirit of revelation and inspiration. He did not complete the publication of this book during his lifetime, but his son, Joseph Smith III, who succeeded him as president of the church, accomplished this in the mid-1860s.

The LDS church publishes its own edition of the King James Version of the Bible, but uses the Inspired Version quite extensively in footnotes even though that version is not accepted as authoritative scripture.

The Book of Mormon is a volume of scripture which Joseph Smith, Jr., translated by the gift and power of God. It contains the story of several peoples who came to America from the Old World and is a religious account of God's dealings with those people. It stands as a witness, along with the Bible, of Jesus Christ.

Many have wondered that there are differences between the editions published by the two churches. For the most part, the texts of both books read the same. There are some slight variations in wording because there were wording differences in the three editions of the Book of Mormon published during Joseph Smith, Jr.'s lifetime. In addition to this, the RLDS church publishes a second version of the Book of Mormon (known as the 1966 edition) in which antiquated words and phraseology were updated to bring it more into line with current language usage. It is not a paraphrased or condensed version.

The main differences between the editions of the Book of Mormon have to do with chapter and verse numbering. This is because the chapter and versification systems developed independently long after the churches had gone their separate ways. In the Appendix there is a cross reference chart which helps readers find the same scriptures in both editions.

A third book of scripture common to both churches is the Doctrine and Covenants. This volume contains the revelations brought to the church by Joseph Smith, Jr., and others.

The LDS church's edition of the Doctrine and Covenants contains 138 sections. With only a few exceptions, the authorship of each of these sections is attributed to Joseph Smith, Jr. The LDS church rarely adds to this volume.

The RLDS church currently (as of 1985) has 156 sections in its Doctrine and Covenants. Joseph Smith, Jr., and each of his successor-prophets have brought these revelations to the church. The RLDS church adds to this volume from time to time, as new messages are brought by the prophet.

There are a number of sections in the LDS edition attributed to Joseph Smith, Jr., which are not used by the RLDS church. Some of these are found in the RLDS church history; the authorship of others is disputed. And, of course, the LDS church does not use any sections brought to the church by the prophets of the RLDS church. Again, a chart in the

Appendix explains the specific sections in this category, as well as providing a comprehensive cross reference to the sections common to both books, but numbered differently. The difference in section numbering is due to the fact that the organization of the books was done after the two churches were separated.

The LDS church uses a fourth book of scripture called The Pearl of Great Price. This book is not used in the RLDS church for a number of reasons: It was not published until 1851—seven years after Joseph Smith's death. It includes the Book of Moses (which is found in Genesis in the Inspired Version of the Bible); the testimony of Joseph Smith, Jr., relating to his first vision, and the organization of the church (which is found in the RLDS *Church History*); Matthew 24 from the Inspired Version of the Bible; the Articles of Faith, a brief statement of belief derived from a letter Joseph Smith, Jr., wrote to a prominent newspaper editor in the 1840s; and the Book of Abraham which purports to be a record written by Abraham and translated from some papyrus scrolls obtained by Joseph Smith in the early 1830s. The Book of Abraham was published in the 1840s in the church paper *Times and Seasons* but the record was never presented to the church by Joseph Smith as scripture. The RLDS church finds a number of doctrinal problems in this work which cannot be reconciled with other scriptures.

SUMMARY

1. The concept of continuing revelation is an important doctrine of the Latter Day Saint churches.

2. The RLDS church sees two methods of revelation as being understood by church members: propo-

sitional—where God communicates the exact wording of the message to the prophet; encounter—where the prophet experiences God, but must formulate the words of the message to transmit it to the members of the church.

3. All messages presented to the RLDS church by the prophet are confirmed by a vote of the church membership in a delegate conference before they are accepted as scripture. On confirmation, the revelations are added to the Doctrine and Covenants.

4. The RLDS church, while confirming the divine calling of the prophetic office, holds that the person occupying that office is still human and capable of making mistakes.

5. The RLDS church uses three books of scripture: the Inspired Version of the Bible, the Book of Mormon, the Doctrine and Covenants.

6. The LDS church believes that God can use different methods to communicate with persons, but that the message will be audibly and verbally communicated.

7. Although the LDS church affirms continuing revelation, these revelations are rarely written down or added to the scriptures.

8. In LDS theology, it is inappropriate for the membership of the church to vote on revelations that the prophet might present.

9. Even though the LDS church abhors the doctrine of infallibility, church members and leaders alike believe that the prophet will never lead the church astray.

10. The LDS church uses four books of scripture: the King James Version of the Bible, the Book of Mormon, the Doctrine and Covenants, and the Pearl of Great Price.

NOTES

1. Duane E. Couey, as quoted in Richard P. Howard, *Restoration Scriptures* (Independence, Missouri: Herald Publishing House, 1969), 13.
2. Sharon Welch, "Revelation in the Restoration Movement," Christian Education Commission, ed., *Restoration: A People Growing* (Independence, Missouri: Herald Publishing House, 1985), 95–96.
3. Ibid., 98.
4. Ibid., 102, 105.
5. RLDS Doctrine and Covenants 25:1b; LDS Doctrine and Covenants 26:2.
6. Peter A. Judd with Clifford A. Cole, *Distinctives: Yesterday and Today* (Independence, Missouri: Herald Publishing House, 1983), 103–104.
7. McConkie, 644.
8. Ibid., 650.
9. Ibid., 150.
10. Edward L. Kimball, ed., *The Teachings of Spencer W. Kimball* (Salt Lake City: Bookcroft, Inc., 1982), 459.

3

PRIESTHOOD

Basic to the RLDS understanding of priesthood is that God has acted and continues to act in human history. At times God intervenes and calls certain individuals or groups of people to specific responsibilities. This call of God, as can be seen in the scriptural record, comes to different people in different ways.

From the early years of the biblical record, the priestly functions of the head of the family and, later, specially appointed persons have played a prominent role in the lives of God's people. Over the years, the functions and relationships of those called to the priesthood have developed and grown as the needs of the people whom those of the priesthood are to serve have changed.

The view that those in the priesthood are to be servants to others is demonstrated clearly by the ministry of Christ. However, as the church grows, it is important that persons be involved in various leadership roles, with specific assignments.

In a recent church publication the RLDS First Presidency has explained this:

First, there were distinctively different kinds of roles for the leadership in the early Christian church as compared with the practices of Judaism. The Old Testament reveals a priesthood which stood between God and humanity, but the New Testament describes leaders who were from among the people and who stood with them. . . .

Second, priesthood was a division of labor and it emerged out of need. Each congregation developed the structure that best suited its particular situation.[1]

In the spring of 1829, Joseph Smith, Jr., records that he, along with Oliver Cowdery, was visited first by John the Baptist and ordained to the Aaronic priesthood, and later ordained under the instruction of Peter, James, and John to the Melchisedec priesthood. The importance of God's role in the priesthood cannot be overemphasized, even though it was not until many years later that the priesthood offices and their related functions we know in the church today were developed. Though some members of the church may be called and ordained to specific priesthood duties, it is important to remember that each member, regardless of priesthood office, is first a Christian and has basic responsibilities in the church.

This idea was affirmed in revelation to Joseph Smith III, in 1887:

All are called according to the gifts of God unto them; and to the intent that all may labor together, let him that laboreth in the ministry and him that toileth in the affairs of men of business and of work labor together with God for the accomplishment of the work intrusted to all.[2]

In the RLDS church the priesthood has always been open to male church members of all races. At times in the church's history there have been periods when additional caution was exercised because of events, such as the American Civil War in the 1860s, when problems could have arisen between slave holders and the church. In any priesthood call the confirmation of the Holy Spirit is essential before any ordination takes place.

The 1984 World Conference of the RLDS church brought new meaning and understanding to priesthood in the revelation given by the prophet Wallace B. Smith. This document addressed a variety of issues of concern and importance to the church, but perhaps none had more impact than the enlightenment concerning priesthood:

Hear, O my people, regarding my holy priesthood. The power of this priesthood was placed in your midst from the earliest days of the rise of this work for the blessing and salvation of humanity. There have been priesthood members over the years, however, who have misunderstood the purpose of their calling. Succumbing to pride, some have used it for personal aggrandizement. Others, through disinterest or lack of diligence, have failed to magnify their calling or have become inactive. When this has happened, the church has experienced a loss of spiritual power, and the entire priesthood structure has been diminished.

It is my will that my priesthood be made up of those who have an abiding faith and desire to serve me with all their hearts, in humility and with great devotion. Therefore, where there are those who are not now functioning in their priesthood, let inquiry be made by the proper administrative officers, according to the provisions of the law, to determine the continuing nature of their commitment.

I have heard the prayers of many, including my servant the prophet, as they have sought to know my will in regard to the question of who shall be called to share the burdens and responsibilities of priesthood in my church. I say to you, now, as I have said in the past, that all are called according to the gifts which have been given them. This applies to priesthood as well as to any other aspects of this work. Therefore, do not wonder that some women of the church are being called to priesthood responsibilities. This is in harmony with my will and where these calls are made known to my servants, they may be processed according to the administrative procedures and provisions of the law. Nevertheless, in the ordaining of women to priesthood, let this be done with all deliberateness. Before the actual laying on of hands takes place, let specific guidelines and instructions be provided by the spiritual authorities, that all may be done in order.[3]

With the acceptance of this revelation by its World Conference, the RLDS church launched an era of new understanding and commitment for the priesthood.

The procedure by which a person is called to

priesthood service is followed carefully: The one responsible for a call attempts to address the needs of the congregation where that person will serve, and also seeks confirmation that God is indeed calling a particular person to a specific function. This call can be discerned by the individual, but cannot be asserted until it has been expressed through others who have administrative responsibilities, as explained by the First Presidency:

First, calls to priesthood are perceived by appropriate adminstrative officers, themselves priesthood called of God. Not just one such officer but at least another must bear testimony of the witness of the Holy Spirit in each call in order for there to be reasonable assurance of the genuineness of this foundational element in priesthood authority.

Second, while weakness will be found in the life of every person called, very private but reasonably comprehensive inquiry is made to assure that the life of each person called is in harmony with the teachings and practices of the church—the body that person shall serve.

Third, with appropriate assurance of the authenticity of the call and the acceptable quality of life, the person is advised of the call and given opportunity to express willingness to serve. Often the Holy Spirit blesses that person with an independent testimony of God's call to him or her, which is very reassuring. Others respond in faith to the general commitment that they have made to serve the Lord to the best of their ability. Either response, from knowledge or faith, is an acceptable response of the individual disciple.

Fourth, after the call, examination, and affirmative response from the individual have occurred, the determination of the acceptance by the people is sought. This is best determined by vote of a conference of the congregation and/or jurisdiction of the church having knowledge of the individual. In cases where the church is not yet planted or sufficiently organized to have a conference, an apostle may act to express the acceptance of the candidate by the church.

Fifth, an additional dimension of the authority of the priesthood members is the competency with which ministry is offered to the body. Both before ordination and after, the quality with which the ministers act "for [persons] in things pertaining to God" commends their ministry to God and the church, and lends it an authority of competence. It is to reinforce this dimension of priesthood authority that standards of preordination and continuing education are being offered.[4]

When these various procedures have been duly completed, a person is ordained by the laying on of hands by those in authority—or in other words, by those who have been previously ordained to the priesthood. Priests in the Aaronic priesthood are able to ordain other members of that priesthood. Elders in the Melchisedec priesthood can ordain persons to that office or any of the Aaronic priesthood offices, etc. It is understood that although authority finally comes from God, it is through the agency of the church that the call is expressed. Priesthood members are held accountable to the church for their conduct and must abide the policies, procedures, and authorities which have been set in place to regulate the affairs of the church.

In response to the call from God in Doctrine and Covenants Section 156, the RLDS church has developed a program of education and priesthood review in order to bring about renewed commitment and dedication to service on the part of priesthood members.

Priesthood members, before ordination, are given the opportunity of completing some basic ministerial education provided by the church in the specific functions of their particular priesthood office. After ordination, they continue their education in order to provide a continually increasing quality of ministry. This education can be obtained through colleges and universities, independent studies, and by various study courses provided by the church. Priesthood members have the right to choose the topics and areas of study that interest them.

Because priesthood is of a continuing nature, and authority has been granted by the church as a privilege, one is expected to enlarge and expand personal gifts in the process of ministry—to magnify one's calling. As a part of this process, the church assists each priesthood member with a priesthood self-evaluation interview.

Every three years, each priesthood member participates in the self-evaluation program with the pastor's guidance. This procedure provides an opportunity for priesthood members to review what they have done in the previous three years, and to commit themselves to a specific plan of service for the next three years. Since priesthood members are free to choose how they respond to their calling, the review process is not an imposition of authority, as some might interpret it.

There is provision for those who are advanced in years, or who have ill health, to be relieved of the day-to-day burdens of ministry and the continuing education requirements, and to function in their priesthood office as their health and desires permit.

The priesthood of the RLDS church consists of two major divisions. The first is the Melchisedec priesthood which includes elders and high priests. The High Priesthood is a term generally applicable when referring to those holding the office of high priest. The president of the church is also the president of the High Priesthood.

The second division is called the Aaronic Order, which consists of the offices of priest, teacher, and deacon. The Presiding Bishop is president of the Aaronic priesthood.

All the general officers of the church—the First Presidency, Council of Twelve Apostles, Presiding Patriarch, Presiding Bishopric—are members of the High Priesthood.

The high priest is charged primarily with pastoral and program administration.

The bishop, an office within the High Priesthood, is charged with financial, custodial, and judicial functions.

An evangelist-patriarch has a special ministry with emphasis on personal counseling, crisis ministry, revivalist evangelism, and the conferring of divine blessing—a patriarchal blessing—through the laying on of hands.

Elders are authorized to perform in the absence of the high priest most of the functions attributed to that office. There are more elders in the church than there are members of any other office.

The Seventy are a ministerial quorum of seventy elders ordained to missionary responsibilities. Church rules provide for seven such quorums. (See the chapter on church administration for further details.)

In the Aaronic priesthood, the priest has local ministerial responsibilities primarily directed toward family functions and relationships. While the members of the Melchisedec priesthood may perform all the ordinances of the church, priests may baptize, administer the sacrament of the Lord's Supper, perform marriages, and ordain others to offices in the Aaronic priesthood. The teacher (different from a church school teacher) is charged with local ministries of reconciliation and revival. A deacon is responsible for local custodial and management functions and with personal ministries related to the welfare and well-being of church members.

With the exception of those priesthood members in full-time ministry, and thus need to be supported by the church, all members of the priesthood and others who function as ministers or in other leadership or instructional capacities do so on their own time and expense.

* * *

While the basics of priesthood, its offices and organization might be similar in the LDS church, the particular office of priesthood takes on additional meaning when one understands that unless a man has been ordained to the Melchisedec priesthood, he is not able to partake fully of the ordinances of the church. Being admitted to the temples of the LDS church to be married, for example, requires that the groom be a member of the Melchisedec priesthood.

The First Presidency of the LDS church has explained it this way:

Priesthood is the power and authority of God delegated to man on earth to act in all things for the salvation of man. By that power our Father created this earth.

He gave the priesthood and the keys to exercise its power to Adam, the first man. Adam, in turn, conferred this priesthood on other men. It has passed from generation to generation.

At times in the history of this earth, the priesthood has been generally removed from among men because of their wickedness.

In 1829, after many centuries of spiritual darkness, the priesthood was restored by heavenly messengers sent by the Lord, and the Church of Jesus Christ was reestablished on the earth.[5]

The extreme importance of the priesthood, and more specifically the Melchisedec priesthood, to

LDS church members is demonstrated by the following statement:

> Everything on earth is subject to the power and authority of the Melchizedek Priesthood....Those who are faithful in their priesthood callings in this life shall continue on in their holy authorizations in eternity....Without the Melchizedek Priesthood salvation in the kingdom of God would not be available for men on earth....This higher priesthood is designed to enable men to gain exaltation in the highest heaven in eternity.[6]

While affirming that priesthood calls come from God, the church makes concerted efforts to see that all adult male members of the church are ordained to the Melchisedec priesthood in order to participate in the temple ceremonies. Prerequisite to ordination is the confirmation by a local church authority that the candidate is worthy to receive the priesthood. In an interview between the candidate and his presiding authority, the candidate must prove that he has a sincere faith in Jesus Christ, in the restored gospel, in the mission of Joseph Smith, and sustain the current president of the church.

A candidate must also be able to show that he is morally clean, prayerful, lives the Word of Wisdom (a code which requires total abstinence from the use of alcohol, tobacco, tea and coffee), pays a full tithing, attends all church meetings, etc.[7]

After the person has been approved for ordination by the local church authorities, his name is presented at a conference for a sustaining vote by the church members in that jurisdiction.

Once ordained, a priesthood member is expected to serve as he is directed by his administrative leaders. Each week a priesthood meeting is conducted at each local ward (congregation) which all priesthood members are expected to attend. Each local jurisdiction is organized by priesthood office. The world church organization provides lesson manuals on an annual basis for each of the priesthood offices. These lessons are taught each week to priesthood members in attendance.

A priesthood member, once ordained, will be a priesthood member throughout his life. Indeed, the church believes that priesthood is eternal, and will continue with that person in the life hereafter. If a member is found to be in transgression, he can either be disfellowshiped from the church—his membership is intact, but he cannot function in the priesthood or partake of the sacraments—or he can be excommunicated, at which time his priesthood becomes null and void.

A former LDS church president has explained priesthood:

As pertaining to man's existence on this earth, priesthood is the power and authority of God delegated to man on earth to act in all things for the salvation of men. It is the power by which the gospel is preached; by which the ordinances of salvation are performed so that they will be binding on earth and in heaven; by which men are sealed up unto eternal life, being assured of the fullness of the Father's kingdom hereafter; and by which in due course the Lord will govern the nations of the earth and all that pertains to them.[8]

In the LDS church, the two divisions of priesthood common to the RLDS church are also present.

The Aaronic priesthood, or the lesser priesthood, is considered preparatory for later responsibility in the Melchisedec priesthood. In general practice all boys age twelve are ordained to the office of deacon in the Aaronic priesthood. Deacons are permitted to serve the emblems of the Lord's Supper.

On reaching the age of fourteen, a boy will be ordained a teacher and assigned to assist a Melchisedec priesthood member in visiting the homes of church members. At age sixteen, boys are usually ordained priests. Priests administer the sacrament of the Lord's Supper, perform baptisms under the direction of their local administrative authority, and can obtain permission to ordain others to offices in the Aaronic priesthood.

Young men who have been active in the church are generally ordained elders in the Melchisedec priesthood on reaching age eighteen.

At nineteen, all males in the church are expected to serve two-year voluntary missions for the church at their own expense. After an interview to determine their worthiness, an application is transmitted to church headquarters, where a specific mission assignment will be given. Before becoming a full-time missionary, a young man must be ordained an elder in the Melchisedec priesthood.

In the Melchisedec priesthood there are the following offices: elder, seventy, high priest, patriarch or evangelist, and apostle. The office of bishop is considered an office in the Aaronic priesthood, but is usually filled by a high priest.

One LDS church writer has stated the following:

It follows that it is greater and more important to hold the Melchizedek priesthood, for instance, than it is to hold any office in that priesthood. It is greater, accordingly, to hold the Melchizedek Priesthood than to hold the office of elder or of an apostle, though, of course, no one could be either an elder or an apostle without first possessing the higher priesthood.

Further, there is no advancement from one office to another within the Melchizedek Priesthood. Every elder holds as much priesthood as an apostle or as the President of the Church, though these latter officers hold greater administrative assignments in the kingdom. . . .

An elder has all the priesthood he needs to qualify for exaltation in the highest heaven of the celestial world. Indeed, when the ordinances of exaltation are performed vicariously in the temples, those for and on whose behalf they are done, have the Melchizedek Priesthood conferred upon them and are ordained elders.[9]

Until 1978 the LDS church would not allow black people to hold the priesthood, but in June of that year, a change in this policy was announced by the First Presidency. Although the text of a revelatory document was never issued, a letter to church leaders and the public affirmed that it was by revelation that the Lord

has confirmed that the long-promised day has come when every faithful, worthy man in the Church may receive the holy priesthood....Accordingly, all worthy male members of the church may be ordained to the priesthood without regard for race or color.[10]

Although women are not allowed to hold priesthood office, the LDS church states that they are entitled to all priesthood blessings.

Those women who go on to their exaltation, ruling and reigning with husbands who are kings and priests, will themselves be queens and priestesses. They will hold positions of power, authority and preferment in eternity.[11]

Former LDS church president Spencer W. Kimball has stated: "The Relief Society is the Lord's organization for women. It complements the priesthood training given to the brethren."[12]

As with the RLDS church, the LDS church also has no paid ministry. Those church leaders who have been called into full-time service for the church, however, are generally supported from church funds.

SUMMARY

1. Both the RLDS and LDS churches are organized according to specific priesthood offices and functions assigned each of those offices.

2. There are two priesthoods, the Melchisedec and the Aaronic.

3. Neither the RLDS nor the LDS church has a paid ministry, although in each church there are full-time church officers who are supported by the church.

4. The RLDS church affirms and emphasizes the responsibilities of the individual member, regardless of priesthood office.

5. In the RLDS belief, the emphasis is placed on an individual's quality of ministry and service to others, rather than particular priesthood office.

6. The RLDS church has never denied priesthood to persons because of race or color.

7. The LDS church reversed its policy of denying priesthood to blacks in 1978.

8. As of 1984, RLDS women may be ordained to priesthood offices.

9. The LDS church does not permit women to hold the priesthood, but has a women's organization which complements the priesthood.

10. Melchisedec priesthood membership in the LDS church is crucial for salvation.

Note: Melchisedec is the name of the high priest to whom Abraham paid his tithes. There are several variant spellings for this name. Throughout this presentation we have used the spelling settled upon by the RLDS church except where quoting directly from LDS publications, which use a variant.

NOTES

1. *Guidelines for Priesthood* (Independence, Missouri: Herald Publishing House, 1985), 13–14.
2. RLDS Doctrine and Covenants 119:8b.
3. Ibid., Section 156.
4. *Guidelines for Priesthood,* 19–20.
5. Melchizedek Priesthood Handbook (Salt Lake City: The Church of Jesus Christ of Latter-day Saints, 1975), 1.
6. McConkie, 476–482.
7. *Melchizedek Priesthood Handbook,* 20.
8. McConkie, 594.
9. Ibid., 596.
10. LDS Doctrine and Covenants, Official Declaration 2.
11. *Gospel Kingdom,* 221–222, 229, as quoted in McConkie, 594.
12. Kimball, 498.

4
CHURCH ADMINISTRATION AND ORGANIZATION

By the time the church was five years old, Joseph Smith, Jr., had established most of the major administrative offices that both the RLDS and LDS churches function with today. Many of these offices had basis in the scriptures. When the church was first organized, the administrative quorums were very basic. With growth, however, a more complex system of government and pastoring has been required.

The First Presidency is the leading quorum in the RLDS church as well as in the LDS church. It is made up of the president of the church, who is also recognized as the prophet, and usually two counselors who are high priests in the Melchisedec priesthood.[1] Over the years in the LDS church there have been occasions when more than two counselors have been brought into service.[2] Each member of the First Presidency is usually assigned administrative responsibility for certain areas of the church program.

In the RLDS church, the president-prophet has the additional responsibility of issuing documents from time to time directing the affairs of the church. These are known as revelations. These special documents are added to the Doctrine and Covenants as directed by the periodic conferences of the church. This has not been done in the LDS church for many years.

There have been occasional exceptions to this in the LDS church. In 1976, the church added two revelations to the canon of scripture, which appear in the LDS Doctrine and Covenants as sections 137 and

138. One of these is an 1836 vision of Joseph Smith, Jr. The other is a 1918 vision given by Joseph F. Smith, then president of the LDS church. A third exception is the 1890 statement by Wilford Woodruff rescinding the practice of polygamy. And finally, there is the 1978 statement notifying members of the church that blacks would be permitted to receive priesthood ordinations. These last two do not appear in the main body of the book, but as appendices called "Official Declarations."[3]

Although in the RLDS church only the president is considered the prophet, seer, and revelator to the church, the LDS church considers all members of the First Presidency to be prophets, seers, and revelators. Counselors in the First Presidency of the LDS church are also ordained as apostles.[4]

Succession in the presidency of the church has been an issue of debate between the two churches for many years. Due to the complex nature of this topic, which is dependent on the interpretation of unclear historical events, we will not attempt to discuss the issue here, except to comment on the methods used by each church.

The RLDS church follows a method whereby the living president appoints his successor. This has been done by way of blessing (in the instance of Joseph Smith, III—see RLDS Doctrine and Covenants, Appendix G); verbally (as was the case with Israel A. Smith); or by document (as was done in the cases of Frederick M. Smith, W. Wallace Smith, and Wallace B. Smith). The basis for this method is found in the RLDS Doctrine and Covenants, Section 43, and LDS Doctrine and Covenants, Section 43.

None else shall be appointed unto this gift [that of directing the church and receiving revelations] except it be through him [referring to Joseph Smith, Jr. or the appointed leader of the church], for if it be taken from him he shall not have power, except to appoint another in his stead.

When the president-prophet of the RLDS church dies or resigns, the First Presidency remains as a functioning quorum until such time as a new president-prophet is ordained, and the quorum of the First Presidency is reorganized.

The LDS church has adopted a method of succession wherein the First Presidency is dissolved at the death of the president, and the Quorum of Twelve Apostles assumes the leadership of the church until one of their number, generally the president of the quorum, is ordained president.[5]

Unlike the RLDS church, which waits for the membership of the church assembled in a conference to give a sustaining vote to the new president before ordination, the LDS church has adopted a procedure whereby the new president is ordained by the Quorum of Twelve Apostles, and the action is sustained by the membership at the next regularly scheduled conference.

In addition, the ordination of the president of the RLDS church has usually taken place during a special public worship service, but the LDS church leadership is ordained in a private ceremony generally conducted in the Salt Lake City temple.

Scriptural basis for the LDS method of succession can be found in the RLDS Doctrine and Covenants, Section 104:11b–d and in the LDS Doctrine and Covenants, Section 107:22–24, which states the following:

Of the Melchisedec priesthood, three presiding high priests, chosen by the body, appointed and ordained to that office, and upheld by the confidence, faith and prayer of the church, form a quorum of the Presidency of the church. The twelve traveling councilors are called to be the Twelve Apostles, or special witnesses of the name of Christ, in all the world; thus differing from other officers in the church in the duties of their calling. And they form a quorum equal in authority and power to the three presidents previously mentioned.

The Council or Quorum of Twelve Apostles is a body common to both churches. This quorum is the "traveling high council" of the church "to officiate in the name of the Lord, under the direction of the Presidency of the church...to build up the church and regulate all the affairs of the same, in all nations."[6]

In the RLDS church, apostles are chosen by revelation given through the prophet. Once the membership of the church has approved the ordination of persons who have been called, they are ordained and take their place in the council. Members of the Quorum of Twelve Apostles in the RLDS church are not sustained as prophets, seers, and revelators, although it is generally recognized that they may seek and receive God's direction in carrying out their specific assignments.

The LDS church considers each member of the Quorum of Twelve Apostles to be a prophet, seer, and revelator. Spencer W. Kimball, former LDS church president, has explained this process:

It is the President of the Church who calls the Apostles, and he is the only one who calls them.... When the individual is chosen, the prophet himself takes it to his counselors, the three of them take it to the Twelve, the (fourteen) of them decide on it all together, unified, never any discordant voice, they accept it, and then he is presented to the Church. He is ordained after he is presented and he is given all the keys that there are in the world—even the keys the President has, except that he holds them in a dormant condition, whereas the President of the Church has them active.[7]

50

In both the RLDS and LDS churches, the presiding bishop is the president of the Aaronic priesthood, and is a high priest in the Melchisedec priesthood. The presiding bishop is responsible for the temporal concerns of the church, which include the tithes and offerings contributed by the membership.[8] The presiding bishop is assisted in this work by two counselors; these three form the Presiding Bishopric.

In the RLDS church, all the bishops of the church belong to the Order of Bishops. The presiding bishop has the responsibility of presiding over the bishops, and calling them together for meetings as needed. The Order of Bishops may present basic financial programs or recommendations to the First Presidency and the World Conference.

The Seventy are assigned to the functions of evangelistic outreach in the church, and although the office is common to both churches, each has taken a somewhat different approach to the organization of the Quorums of Seventy.

At the 1982 World Conference, the RLDS church, acting on the scriptural directive and qualifications found in Doctrine and Covenants 104:43 (LDS 107:93–98), fully organized the seven Quorums of Seventy as provided for. Each of the seven quorums is assigned to a geographical region of the church. Each may have a total of seventy members. One member of each of the seven quorums is chosen as the president of that quorum. The seven presidents make up the Council of Seven Presidents of Seventy, with one selected as the senior president, who presides over the meetings of that council. Many of the seventy are full-time appointed church leaders. A growing number of the seventy, however, work in their home areas on a part-time basis, providing their own financial support.

The LDS church has organized a "seventies quorum" in each of the stakes of the church, now numbering over 1,000.[9] Among the ranks of the general leadership of the church is the First Quorum of Seventy. This is the only quorum of seventy where the members are full-time church leaders. In the April 1984 conference of the LDS church, a new arrangement for members of this quorum was announced, where many called into this quorum will serve for a period of from three to five years, rather than for life as in the past.[10] Seven members of the first quorum are chosen as presidents who preside over the first quorum and all other Quorums of Seventy in the church.[11]

The presiding evangelist-patriarch is the president of the Order of Evangelist-Patriarchs in the RLDS church, and as such gives leadership in the training of evangelists who have been called to serve the church in their local areas. They are responsible for giving patriarchal blessings and other spiritual and evangelistic ministry as they perceive a need. They do not have administrative responsibilities. The office of the presiding patriarch is the repository for all patriarchal blessings given to church members.

In 1979 the presiding patriarch in the LDS church was released from active service and given the honorary title of Presiding Patriarch Emeritus. No one else has been called to replace him nor is likely to be. Since stakes have been organized in virtually all parts of the world, and patriarchs have been called to serve in these stakes, there was no longer a need for a patriarch to the church, since his main function was to give blessings to church members who did not have access to a local patriarch.[12]

Unique to the RLDS church is the Standing High Council, which is made up of twelve high priests appointed by the First Presidency and sustained by the World Conference. This body meets at the request of the First Presidency to consider questions of moral and ethical significance, to approve certain ordinations, and to consider appeals from local church courts and other judicial matters.

Although each stake of the LDS church has a quorum of high priests, the RLDS church has one Quorum of High Priests, which includes all high priests in the church who are not members of other quorums or orders. A president of the High Priests Quorum, with two counselors, is appointed by the First Presidency.

Since the organization of the church in 1830, periodic conferences involving a representative body of the entire church membership have been conducted. In the early years of the church these were held by notice; later they were convened twice yearly, in April and October. As the church grew and its needs began to change, conferences were held just once a year and finally, in the mid-1930s, it was decided to have a World Conference every two years. In the RLDS church, the World Conference brings delegates together from all over the world for a week to consider the church budget, act on resolutions from various jurisdictions, inspired documents from the prophet, and other concerns of the general church organization which require the approval of the general membership. Committee reports mandated by previous conferences are received, and worship services, including preaching, prayer meetings, and Communion, are provided.

The LDS church continues to hold its World General Conference in April and October each year, generally for two days each time. Except for a brief business session during one of the conference meetings, wherein members of the church can sustain the general church leaders, the entire conference is devoted to listening to sermons delivered by a number of the leading authorities of the church: the First Presidency, Twelve Apostles, and First Quorum of Seventy.

One prominent LDS church leader has explained that

conferences are far more than religious conventions in which views are expressed, differences resolved, and policies adopted. Rather they consist in a series of meetings at which the mind and will of the Lord is manifest to the people by the mouths of his servants. The Church being a kingdom, not a democracy, instruction and direction comes from above; it does not originate with the citizens but with the king.[13]

This viewpoint can be contrasted with the RLDS church's view of the principle of common consent wherein

the people have the right to share in the selection of their leaders through the democratic process of elections, approval of appointments, and other legislative procedures. They also have the right at each administrative level to help decide the policies and programs at that level. Issues subject to legislative action include such matters as inspired documents directed to the church as a whole and to the world, financial appropriations, the sustaining of ordained leaders, and the election of various officers.[14]

A major administrative division of the RLDS church is the Region. The 1972 World Conference provided that "regions may be organized for legislative and educational functions where it is desirable or necessary to facilitate the work of the church."[15]

Regions may include stakes, districts, and other developmental areas, and are directed by either a regional administrator or a regional president, depending on the needs of the church in a particular area. Each region has a bishop or bishop's agent assigned to represent the functions of the Presiding Bishopric in the local area. The regional president or administrator reports directly to the apostle in charge of the field jurisdiction which includes the region.

On July 1, 1984, the LDS church introduced an ad ministrative jurisdiction known as an Area. The church was divided into thirteen major geographical areas— seven in the United States and Canada, and six in other parts of the world. Each area is directed by a president and two counselors, appointed from among the members of the First Quorum of Seventy. The area presidencies are accountable to the First Presidency and the Council of Twelve for building up the church and regulating affairs in their respective areas.[16]

Both churches have Stake jurisdictions. A stake, generally an association of several congregations, is organized in geographic areas of relatively high density of church membership. The stake presidency presides over the stake and is administratively responsible for all stake activities. Stake presidents are appointed by the Joint Council of First Presidency, Council of Twelve, and Presiding Bishopric in the RLDS church, and approved by members of the stake. The stake president chooses two counselors from among the high priests of the stake to assist him in administering the church program.

Each stake has a Stake High Council, composed of twelve high priests. The high council assists the Stake Presidency, and is the highest judicial body in the stake, with both original and appellate jurisdiction.

In the RLDS church, the stake bishop, with two counselors, is the chief financial officer in the stake. The stake bishop is responsible to the stake conference for all stake finances and for the physical management of stake properties. The stake bishopric also represents the Presiding Bishopric in the stake.

With two exceptions, the LDS stake organization is very similar. In the LDS church there is no stake bishop. The financial affairs of the stake are administered by the stake president. LDS stakes are associations of several wards.[17]

The RLDS congregation and the LDS ward are similar in nature. A congregation is directed by a pastor, or presiding elder, with counselors as the size of the congregation and its needs might dictate. The LDS ward is presided over by a bishop, with two counselors. This ward bishopric is responsible for both the spiritual and temporal affairs of the members of the ward.[18]

In the lesser developed areas of the church, both the RLDS and LDS churches are organized into districts, presided over by a district president, with two counselors. The districts are associations of branches. In the RLDS church branches are directed by a pastor, often referred to as presiding elder or branch president, with counselors as needs dictate. The LDS branches are administered by a branch president, with two counselors.[19]

SUMMARY

1. The RLDS church and the LDS church have similar administrative quorums, with significant functional differences.

2. In RLDS practice, the president of the church is also the prophet—designated as the one person to receive and issue revelations from God to the church.

3. In LDS belief, the president of the church serves a similar function as that of the RLDS church, but additional general church leaders are ceremonially sus-

tained by church members as prophets, seers, and revelators.

4. RLDS church presidents are designated by their immediate predecessor, to succeed on death or resignation.

5. LDS church presidents have traditionally been selected from the Quorum of Twelve Apostles; the president of the quorum becoming church president on the death of a president.

6. The Presiding Bishopric is responsible for the financial concerns of each church.

7. In both churches, the Presiding Bishop is president of the Aaronic priesthood.

8. The Seventy are charged with missionary duties, but each church has approached the organization of the Quorums of Seventy somewhat differently.

9. Unique to the RLDS church is the Presiding Evangelist-Patriarch. This officer presides over all other evangelist-patriarchs in the church.

10. Patriarchs are ordained at the local level in the LDS church, but as of 1979 there is no longer a Presiding Patriarch in the church.

11. The RLDS church conducts its affairs at a biennial World Conference. Church members receive instruction from leaders and have a voice in church legislation affecting administrative matters. Various spiritual matters are also handled by Conference action.

12. LDS conferences are occasions for church members to receive instruction from leaders. Direction in the administration of the church is usually not discussed.

13. A major ecclesiastical organization in each church is the stake—an association of congregations.

14. In both churches, the stake is administered by a stake president and two counselors. Each stake has a

Stake High Council, composed of no more than twelve high priests.

15. Stakes in the RLDS church have a Stake Bishopric, which administers the finances of the stake and represents the functions of the Presiding Bishopric at the local level.

NOTES

1. RLDS Doctrine and Covenants 104:11a, b; LDS Doctrine and Covenants 107:21–22.
2. *1985 Church Almanac*, 46–47.
3. Ibid., 104, 106.
4. LeGrand Richard, A. *Marvelous Work and a Wonder* (Salt Lake City: Deseret Book Co., 1976), 135–136; McConkie, 651.
5. McConkie, 591, 49.
6. RLDS Doctrine and Covenants 104:12; LDS Doctrine and Covenants 107:33.
7. Kimball, 468; McConkie, 646.
8. RLDS Doctrine and Covenants 104:32, 33; LDS Doctrine and Covenants 107:68–74.
9. Richards, 162.
10. *1985 Church Almanac*, 128.
11. McConkie, 282.
12. *Ensign*, November 1979, p. 18 (Official magazine of the Church of Jesus Christ of Latter-day Saints.)
13. McConkie, 155–56.
14. *Church Administrators Handbook* (Independence, Missouri: Herald Publishing House, 1980), 12.
15. *1982 Supplement to Rules and Resolutions*, paragraph 31, p. 14.
16. *1985 Church Almanac*, 296–302.
17. Richards, 162.
18. Ibid., 163.
19. Ibid.

5

SALVATION

The principle of salvation is perhaps one of the most important—but the most difficult—beliefs to comprehend. The Basic Beliefs Committee summarized the RLDS belief regarding salvation:

> We believe that humans cannot be saved in the kingdom of God except by the grace of the Lord Jesus Christ, who loves us while we are yet in our sins, and who gave his life to reconcile us to God. Through this atonement of the Lord Jesus Christ and by the gift of the Holy Spirit, persons receive power to choose God and to commit their lives to God; thus are they turned from rebellion, healed from sin, renewed in spirit, and transformed after the image of God in righteousness and holiness.[1]

Salvation as a gift from God is the most profound statement of his love for humankind. This love which is shared by Christ is difficult to describe. It is equally difficult to attempt to put limits on what God has done for persons everywhere.

We are able to obtain brief glimpses of God's love from the testimonies of many people. We can learn of this love from what we know of Christ's mortal ministry. Through these experiences we can come to know something of what it means to be loved even though we are sinful.

The Basic Beliefs Committee has attempted to explain God's purpose in Christ:

> When the followers of Christ have remained true to the faith they have known and borne testimony to the fact that "God is in Christ, reconciling the world unto himself" [II Corinthians 5:19]. While the mystery of this reconciling power reaches beyond our comprehension we do know of his transforming presence in the lives of his disciples. From Magdalene to Paul to us, men who have been at war within themselves, in rebellion against God,

and both hating and exploiting their fellows have suddenly become new men as they sensed the grace of God through the Lord Jesus Christ and yielded their lives to him. Then, being renewed by the Holy Spirit, they have been able to do what the law commanded (i.e., to love God with all their hearts and their neighbors as themselves) which they had never been able to do previously. Where once they rationalized and justified their own sin and inadequacy, under the reconciling power of God they found their lives were changed, so much so that now they say in glad response, "We have been changed from death unto life". . . .

No man can really find peace with himself or with his neighbors or with the universe until he is reconciled to God. The power for such reconciliation is resident in Jesus Christ who is our mediator, the Word made flesh which dwelt among us in grace and truth.[2]

Jesus Christ came to earth, lived and taught, and then gave his life for all persons. His ministry and his sacrifice have given us hope that life is eternal. We learn from his teachings and the witness of the Holy Spirit that the resurrection is a historical reality and that each person will participate in this great gift.

The RLDS church believes that it is Jesus Christ who saves humankind, and that significant aspects of the salvation process may occur through the ministry of the church.

Men and women are responsible and accountable to God for what they do during their lives. The Basic Beliefs Committee of the RLDS church has this to say:

There is no question about whether or not the church has a viable role in the saving process. *It does!* [Ephesians 4:12, 13]. Or whether or not its people participate in the saving experience. *They do!* [Matthew 28:18–19; Acts 2:38, 39]. Or whether or not baptized people are saved. If they believe in Jesus Christ and are committed to him, *they are!"* [John 3:3–5].[3]

Members of the RLDS church have come to know that education and salvation are not options that are terminated by death. There is no question that it is the grace of Jesus Christ that makes this option possible, either before or after the grave.

In his first letter, Peter tells us that

Christ also once suffered for sins, the just for the unjust, being put to death in the flesh, but quickened by the Spirit, that he might bring us to God. For which cause also, he went and preached unto the spirits in prison. . . . The gospel is preached to them who are dead, that they might be judged according to men in the flesh, but live in the spirit according to the will of God.[4]

The implications of this passage were given greater meaning in a vision given to Joseph Smith, Jr., where he saw the celestial kingdom of God. Joseph writes that he saw his brother Alvin (who had died before the church was organized) and

marveled how it was that he had obtained an inheritance in that kingdom, seeing that he had departed this life before the Lord had set his hand to gather Israel the second time, and had not been baptized for the remission of sins.

Thus came the voice of the Lord unto me, saying: "All who have died without a knowledge of this gospel, who would have received it if they had been permitted to tarry, shall be heirs of the celestial kingdom of God; also all that shall die henceforth without a knowledge of it, who would have received it with all their hearts, shall be heirs of that kingdom.

"For I, the Lord, will judge all men according to their works, according to the desire of their hearts."

And I also beheld that all children who die before they arrive at the years of accountability, are saved in the celestial kingdom of heaven.[5]

This concept is also supported by and further explained in the Book of Mormon by Moroni:

For, behold, all little children are alive in Christ, and also all they that are without the law.

For the power of redemption comes on all that have no law; wherefore, he that is not condemned, or he that is under no condemnation, cannot repent; and to such baptism avails nothing.[6]

This understanding from the scriptures differs greatly from the LDS church belief that even those who are dead must still be baptized, confirmed, and (if male) ordained to the Melchisedec priesthood, in order to obtain exaltation in the celestial kingdom. These ordinances are performed by a living person on behalf of the one who is dead.

In this life those who hear the gospel and repent should commit their lives to Christ in baptism by immersion in water. Baptism is a sacred ordinance filled with many symbolisms. There is the burial in water of the old life and the coming forth of the new. There is the cleansing agent of the water, symbolically washing away sins. Later those baptized can receive the ministry of the Holy Spirit through the laying on of hands by those recognized by the church as having authority to do so.

The RLDS church teaches that

man yields himself to his Lord because he knows the love of God for him, personally, and thus claims the marvelous gift of forgiveness. While this does not make a person sinless nor even free from all the results of sin, it does free him from the burden of guilt and allows him to respond wholeheartedly to the direction of the Holy Spirit. The knowledge of sin forgiven can be a strengthening factor to the human spirit.

Eternal life, as Jesus said, is to know God and his Son Jesus Christ. It is partaking of the nature of Jesus Christ—becoming more like him. And this transformation of life comes only through the experience of forgiveness made possible by feeling the love of Christ and surrendering to him. The reconciled, committed person lives in faithful obedience to the will of God and in his obedience develops an eternal quality of life. This is the promise of God in Jesus Christ.[7]

Closely related to, and the conclusion of, the salvation process is the judgment. The RLDS church believes in eternal judgment and that through this judgment God will determine a person's destiny according to his divine wisdom and love, and according to the response of the person to God's call.

Because Latter Day Saints believe that all the circumstances and conditions of all lives are known to God, this judgment is just and merciful. God deals with each person on an individual basis.

Such wisdom and purpose is only dimly perceived by men even when they are at their best. The mysteries of eternity almost always remain mysteries. This does not mean that men do not comprehend God; it means that they are never able to comprehend God fully.[8]

In the RLDS Doctrine and Covenants Section 76 (same in LDS Doctrine and Covenants) Joseph Smith, Jr., has given us a detailed explanation of this process, and some metaphors regarding personal glory after the judgment.[9]

* * *

A distinction that separates the doctrine of the LDS church from most others is the definition of the difference between salvation and exaltation. Many observers have become confused at this; they question whether the LDS church believes that salvation is a gift from God. Part of the questioning is due to the fact that in the past years, the LDS church has emphasized its institution and the good works required to be a good member.

The LDS church teaches that all people were created as spirits in the premortal existence, and that those spirits were infused into physical bodies created by mortal parents here on earth.

When death occurs, the body is disposed of and the spirit of the person goes to the spirit world. It was to this place that Christ went to preach the gospel during the time from his death until the resurrection. It was this experience that was referred to in I Peter 3:18–19; 4:6.

After the resurrection everyone will be judged, and assigned a place for eternity in one of three places: the celestial kingdom, where God and Christ rule; the terrestrial kingdom where Christ will be present; or the telestial kingdom where only the presence of the Holy Spirit will be enjoyed.

The LDS church teaches that while all will receive salvation, salvation without exaltation is damnation.[10] The late LDS apostle LeGrand Richard has explained this:

James [in the New Testament] makes it clear that to believe in God is not sufficient, for the devils do as much, and that "faith without works is dead." A farmer might just as well believe that he can harvest a crop without planting. Such faith is dead; it will not produce a harvest without works....

How useless is one's faith without works! What a glorious award awaits those who deal profitably with the talents they receive! How inconsistent is the thought that all who do good are rewarded alike, and all who do evil are punished alike! How difficult it would be to draw the line between the two groups! Hence, the need for "many mansions" in our Father's kingdom, where each will be rewarded according to his works.[11]

The late apostle Bruce R. McConkie has stated the following:

One of the untrue doctrines found in modern Christendom is the concept that man can gain salvation [meaning in the kingdom of God] by grace alone and without obedience....Immortality is a free gift....Salvation in the celestial kingdom of God, however, is not salvation by grace alone. Rather, it is salvation by grace coupled with obedience to the laws and ordinances of the gospel.[12]

Celestial marriage, discussed elsewhere in this volume, is seen by the LDS church as the only way by which people can obtain exaltation which consists of the eternity of the family unit. Those who obtain this exaltation gain an inheritance in the highest of the three heavens within the celestial kingdom.[13]

The LDS church bases many of its teachings, including those regarding salvation and marriage, on ideas taught by Joseph Smith, Jr., during the latter few years of his life. Many of these concepts, which RLDS church members find unacceptable, were never presented to the church for a sustaining vote. Baptism for the dead is one such concept. (The differences between the two churches in the manner of the prophetic office are discussed at length elsewhere in this volume.)

The LDS church's belief in regard to salvation for the dead is published in a missionary tract:

God being no respecter of persons, it would be manifestly unjust for one portion of the human family to have the privilege of hearing the gospel in this life, while a great proportion never heard it and lay under condemnation for the fact. No, the plan of salvation is complete; it reaches from our premortal state, applies to our present condition, and extends to our future state, until every son or daughter of father Adam has had ample opportunity to embrace its tenets and live in accordance with its spirit. . . .

Great numbers of those who have gone into the spirit world have never submitted to the ordinance of baptism, while vast numbers of those who were baptized had the ordinance administered by one who held no rightful authority and whose acts God will not recognize.

They stand in the same position to the kingdom of God as does a man who, as an alien to the government of a country, has received his papers of citizenship from someone who held no office under the government and, as a consequence, had no authority to confer these rights upon anyone.[14]

(*Note:* The implication here is that only the priesthood of the LDS church is recognized by God.)

The LDS church seeks to establish biblical

precedent for the ordinance of baptism for the dead, and in addition to that, all other ordinances it has deemed necessary (as noted above) for salvation, with a passage found in I Corinthians 15:29: "Else what shall they do which are baptized for the dead, if the dead rise not at all? Why are they then baptized for the dead?"

It is believed that those who do the vicarious work for the dead become "saviors upon Mount Zion."[15]

These sacred ordinances performed by faithful LDS church members on behalf of the dead can be done only in the temples which the church has built in many places around the world. (Temples and their related purposes and meanings will be discussed elsewhere in this volume.)

The doctrine of salvation for the dead has been summed up as follows:

> The great principles and procedures whereby the saving truths of the gospel are offered to, accepted by, and made binding upon the departed dead, comprise the doctrine of salvation for the dead. Pursuant to this doctrine the principles of salvation are taught in the spirit world, leaving the ordinances thereof to be performed in this life on a vicarious-proxy basis. By accepting the gospel in the spirit world, and because the ordinances of salvation and exaltation are performed vicariously in this world, the worthy dead can become heirs of the fulness of the Father's kingdom. Salvation for the dead is the system whereunder those who would have accepted the gospel in this life had they been permitted to hear it, will have the chance to accept it in the spirit world, and will then be entitled to all the blessings which passed them by in mortality.[16]

It is for this reason that the LDS church has become widely known for its genealogical research efforts and facilities.

SUMMARY

1. Salvation in the kingdom of God comes to all humankind through the grace of Christ.

2. We can learn of God's love for the human race from what we know of Christ's mortal ministry.

3. Christ's ministry and sacrifice give hope that life can be eternal.

4. The RLDS church believes that it is Jesus Christ who saves.

5. Members of the RLDS church believe that education and salvation are not options that are terminated by death.

6. Joseph Smith, Jr., wrote that those who died without receiving the gospel will be saved in the celestial glory with God.

7. The LDS church makes a distinction between salvation and exaltation.

8. In the LDS church, salvation comes through the grace of Christ, coupled with obedience to the laws and ordinances of the gospel.

9. The LDS church believes that marriages must be performed in its temples, and that only those so married will be exalted in the highest degree of the celestial kingdom of God.

10. Unique to the teachings of the LDS church are those that require living persons to be baptized, ordained, and "sealed" on behalf of dead persons who did not know of the church during their lives.

NOTES

1. *A Believing People* (Independence, Missouri: Herald Publishing House, 1977), 6. A brochure produced by the Evangelism Commission of the RLDS church.
2. *Exploring the Faith,* 110–11.
3. Ibid., 107.
4. I Peter 3:18–19; 4:6.
5. RLDS *Church History,* Vol. 2 (Independence, Missouri: Herald Publishing House, 1952), 16; LDS Doctrine and Covenants 137.
6. Book of Mormon, Moroni 8:25–26.
7. *Exploring the Faith,* 124–125.
8. Ibid., 230.
9. For further information regarding RLDS beliefs about salvation see Clifford A. Cole, *The Mighty Act of God* (Independence, Missouri: Herald Publishing House, 1984), ch. 9.
10. Richards, 263.
11. Ibid., 268–69.
12. McConkie, 669.
13. Ibid., 257.
14. *Plan of Salvation* (Salt Lake City: The Church of Jesus Christ of Latter-day Saints, 1983), 20–21.
15. Ibid., 23.
16. McConkie, 673.

6

MARRIAGE

Basic to the beliefs of most Christian churches is the sanctity of the marriage covenant. Such is the case with both the RLDS and LDS churches.

Early in its history, the church and its members affirmed that marriage was sacred. This statement, found today in Section 111 of the Doctrine and Covenants, was formulated by church leaders and accepted unanimously at a church conference held in 1835. (This section is no longer found in the LDS church edition of the Doctrine and Covenants. It was removed from the 1876 edition, having been replaced with a section regarding plural marriage. This will be discussed later.)

Section 111 continues to guide the RLDS church's understanding of the marriage covenant, and gives guidelines on procedures for the ceremony and meanings of the relationship.

The RLDS church recognizes the civil authorities in these matters and understands that some governments have regulations which would preclude RLDS ministers from performing the marriage ceremony. However, in many of the nations where the church is functioning, any member of the Melchisedec priesthood, or a priest in the Aaronic priesthood, is given authority by the church to perform marriage ceremonies.

The marriage ceremony is a special worship service, usually conducted in the church, to which friends and family are invited.

Considered a sacrament of the church, the marriage covenant has been explained as follows:

The act and state of marriage have their origins in the scriptures as being instituted by God. In Genesis we read, "And the Lord God said, It is not good that the man should be alone; I will make an help meet for him," [see Genesis 2:18 KJV, 2:23, 24 IV] and "Therefore shall a man leave his father and his mother, and shall cleave unto his wife; and they shall be one flesh." [See Genesis 2:24; 2:30 IV.] The basic statement in the Doctrine and Covenants is "Whoso forbiddeth to marry, is not ordained of God, for marriage is ordained of God unto man; wherefore it is lawful that he should have one wife, and they twain shall be one flesh, and all this that the earth might answer the end of its creation; and that it might be filled with the measure of man, according to his creation before the world was made." [See Doctrine and Covenants 49:3a–c; LDS section 49.]

Not only is God seen as endorsing marriage in principle; divine action is also evident in each specific union of two persons in the marriage ceremony. Doctrine and Covenants 111 indicates that after vows have been exchanged, the minister "shall pronounce them 'husband and wife' in the name of the Lord Jesus Christ." [See Doctrine and Covenants 111:2c.] In the Bible Jesus is recorded as saying in connection with marriage and divorce, "What, therefore, God hath joined together, let no man put asunder." [See Matthew 19:6; Mark 10:9 (10:7 IV.] In the marriage ceremony, the minister acts on behalf of God in joining together a man and a woman.

Marriage is a covenant. The covenant is made between the two individuals in the presence of God and of the church as witness. The words, "You both mutually agree to be each other's companion..." [Doctrine and Covenants 111:2b], indicate the nature of the marriage covenant. It is a commitment to companionship, mutual support, shared responsibility, and love toward each other. The marriage covenant has as its ideal the depth and integrity which characterize God's covenant relationship with humanity. The sacramental nature of the marriage covenant derives from its relationship to God's covenant with persons. Furthermore, in marriage two individuals embark on a covenant relationship in which they commit themselves to express their best understanding of the demands of Christian discipleship.

Marriage in the church is considered a lifelong commitment as indicated by the phrase "during your lives" (Doctrine and Covenants 111:2b) which is required as a part of each wedding ceremony in the church. This understanding of marriage as a lifelong commitment is the reason why divorce is to be avoided. Prior to Joseph Smith's death in 1844 speculation regarding the eternal nature of marriage was present within the church. The Reorganized church has always rejected the view that marrige covenants are valid after death. One might suppose that speculation about eternal marriage is based in part at least on Jesus' statements that "whatsoever thou shalt bind on earth, shall be bound in heaven" [Matthew 16:19; 16:20 IV] and "In the resurrection, they neither marry, nor are given in marriage." [Matthew 22:30; 22:29 IV.][1]

That the marriage covenant is one of the most sacred commitments made by a church member is seen in the church's firm stance on adultery. Adultery is considered to be a violation of the marriage covenent, and is one of the few grounds for a church court trial.

The RLDS church recognizes that there are those who, for various reasons, have had to terminate a marriage. Because the incidence of divorce in our society has become more frequent, the church has responded by providing a means whereby divorced persons can obtain the church's permission to remarry. In these cases the church tries to proceed with care and caution.

In the past, one of the major points of disagreement between the RLDS church and the LDS church had to do with polygamy. The arguments focused on whether or not Joseph Smith, Jr., was involved in its practice. Unfortunately, historical documents presently available seem to provide support for both sides of the issue, with neither being definitive. Some members of the RLDS church assert that Joseph Smith was not involved in polygamy just as firmly as LDS members assert that he was.

Most important, however, is that Joseph Smith, Jr.,

publicly denounced the doctrine and removed people from the church for practicing polygamy or advocating its practice. Numerous published statements in the church paper at Nauvoo, the *Times and Seasons*, support this public stance of denial.[2]

The RLDS church affirms that, Joseph Smith's private actions aside, the Book of Mormon and the Doctrine and Covenants promote monogamy, while denouncing other kinds of marital relationships. The scriptures contain the guidelines for doctrine and faith, and the RLDS church takes a position that if doctrines or actions are not in harmony with the scriptures, then those doctrines or actions are not correct.

This understanding of the marital relationship gave cause for reflection by many church members when missionary work began among certain peoples in Third World nations. There were some who, because of their culture and previous religious understandings, were involved in polygamous marriages. Because these families had been well established, the church was required to reinterpret its stance. This understanding allows the church to minister to these people and teach them the Christian way of life, leading them into monogamy, successfully.

In a revelation to the church during its concern over this situation, the prophet W. Wallace Smith wrote the following:

Monogamy is the basic principle on which Christian married life is built. Yet, as I have said before, there are also those who are not of this fold to whom the saving grace of the gospel must go.

When this is done the church must be willing to bear the burden of their sin, nurturing them in the faith, accepting that degree of repentance which it is possible for them to achieve, looking forward to the day when through patience and love they can be free as a people from the sins of the years of their ignorance.[3]

* * *

The LDS church position on marriage maintains many of the basic tenets which are understood by most Christian churches. There are some major differences, however, which make their understanding unique.

Today the LDS church no longer permits polygamy, but for a number of years in the 1800s was well-known for its practice. Although Section 132 is still printed in the LDS Doctrine and Covenants, the practice of plural marriage was suspended in 1890 by LDS president Wilford Woodruff. There are several LDS fundamentalist groups in Utah and the surrounding areas which continue the practice of polygamy. These members have been removed from the LDS church.

The eternity of the marriage covenant is basic to the LDS beliefs and the ultimate goal of church members. Various scriptures are interpreted by LDS leaders as supporting the idea that the family unit continues forever, if that unit has been properly sealed in a temple of the church.

A prominent LDS church leader and theologian writes:

> Marriages performed in the temples for time and eternity, by virtue of the sealing keys restored by Elijah, are called celestial marriages. The participating parties become husband and wife in this mortal life, and if after their marriage they keep all the terms and conditions of this order of the priesthood, they continue on as husband and wife in the celestial kingdom of God.
>
> If the family unit continues, then by virtue of that fact the members of the family have gained eternal life (exaltation), the greatest of all the gifts of God, for by definition exaltation consists in the continuation of the family unit in eternity.[4]

The late LDS apostle LeGrand Richards, in what has become one of the best-selling LDS books and basic for the study of the church's missionaries, explains the church's position further:

> The Lord intended that the marriage covenant should be for time and for all eternity, and the practice of marrying "until death do you part" did not originate with the Lord or his servants, but is a man-made doctrine. Therefore, all men and women who have died without having been sealed to each other for time and for all eternity, by the power of the holy priesthood, have no claim upon their children, for the children have not been born under the covenant of eternal marriage.[5]

Eternal marriages can be performed only in the temples of the LDS church and only by specially designated members of the Melchisedec priesthood.

Other ecclesiastical authorities can perform civil marriages, depending on the local laws, but these marriages are only for time. Worthy church members can later have their marital relationship "sealed" in the temple for eternity.

Although marriages for time can be performed in the temples under certain circumstances, the general policy is that a man can be sealed for eternity to more than one woman, but a woman may only be sealed to one man. The LDS prophet is the only one who has authority to cancel a sealing and then it is done only under certain special circumstances.

Many LDS church members believe that temple marriages are less likely to result in divorce, as evidenced by the following statement of the late LDS church president Spencer W. Kimball: "For marriages performed outside the temples, the threat of divorce is much greater."[6]

Because its missionary program takes many thousands of young men and women into other cultural areas, interracial marriage has received some attention from LDS church leaders over the years. Although the church does not condemn interracial relationships, nor do they attach any sinful stigma to them, church leaders have strongly recommended that members avoid these kinds of marriages:

We are unanimous, all of the Brethren [meaning general church leaders], in feeling and recommending that Indians marry Indians, and Mexicans marry Mexicans; the Chinese marry Chinese and the Japanese marry Japanese; that the Caucasians marry the Caucasians, and the Arabs marry Arabs.[7]

SUMMARY

1. The RLDS church and the LDS church both affirm the sanctity of the marriage covenant.

2. The RLDS church understands that monogamy is the basic Christian lifestyle.

3. Members of the Melchisedec priesthood and priests of the Aaronic Order in the RLDS church can perform marriages, subject to local civil laws.

4. The RLDS church interprets the scriptures to mean that the marriage covenant as understood in this life does not continue in the next, but a different relationship prevails.

5. Marriages are generally performed by RLDS ministers in the church buildings in a public ceremony.

6. The LDS church understands that though monogamy is the prevailing marital lifestyle, polygamy once was permitted by God as an authorized relationship.

7. The LDS church condemns the practice of polygamy today.

8. LDS marriages which are perfomed in its temples, are not only for this life, but the life hereafter.

9. LDS practices permit more than one wife to be sealed to a man.

10. The LDS church believes that the family unit as constituted in this life, can continue for eternity.

11. Both churches base their beliefs on teachings and historical evidences from the scriptures and from Joseph Smith, Jr., even though the interpretations of events and documents are different.

NOTES

1. *The Priesthood Manual*, 251–53.
2. *Times and Seasons* 5:474; 5:490; *Nauvoo Neighbor*, June 19, 1844; *LDS Church History* 6:410–411.
3. RLDS Doctrine and Covenants 150:10.
4. McConkie, 117.
5. Richards, 188.
6. Kimball, 297.
7. Ibid., 303.

7

THE TEMPLE

Ever since 1831, when Joseph Smith, Jr., and other church leaders dedicated a tract of land in Independence, Missouri, members of the RLDS church have been longing for the day when a temple could be erected and its ministries enjoyed.

Because of persecution in the early 1830s, Latter Day Saint believers were unable to build a temple in Independence, but later were successful in the construction of a "House of the Lord" at Kirtland, Ohio, which was dedicated in 1836.

This "House of the Lord," or the "Kirtland Temple" as it came to be known, was intended as a public house of worship, and it continues to be used in this manner under the ownership of the RLDS church. This structure was also to provide a facility for the functions of the general church leaders and for studies relating to their responsibilities by the various priesthood quorums of the church.

The RLDS church accepts temple functions as ministries to the living, which should

emphasize *edification* rather than *exaltation, dedication* rather than *adoration,* "life before death" rather than "life after death." It would be for the developing of flesh-and-blood Saints who live here and now rather than celestialized Saints for lands and times hereafter.[1]

In a 1968 editorial, the RLDS First Presidency called church members to

think of the temple as a place where those who are called to share in the ministry of Jesus meet with each other and God to ask hard questions about the demands of redemptive ministry. Let us find there the spiritual resources which make possible such sacrificial and redemptive ministry. Let us go there for enrichment and refreshment only to go out and spend our riches and release our power on behalf of suffering humanity.

The Temple of Zion must represent more than anything else the spirit of Zion of which the ancient prophet said of the purpose of God:

"And he will teach us of his ways, and we will walk in his paths: for out of Zion shall go forth the law, and the word of the Lord from Jerusalem. And he shall judge among the nations, and they shall rebuke many people; and they shall beat their swords into plowshares, and their spears into pruning hooks: nation shall not lift up sword against nation, neither shall they learn war any more."

[If] the temple of Zion serves this function. . .it not only will contribute to human redemption through the specific activities which are carried on there but will be a church-wide symbol of the divine mission of the church to the world to make contemporary application of divine intelligence to human needs.[2]

The long-awaited day for the construction of a temple in Independence began to unfold in 1968. RLDS church president W. Wallace Smith brought a revelation to the church which made reference to the temple:

The time has come for a start to be made toward building my temple in the Center Place. It shall stand on a portion of the plot of ground set apart for this purpose many years ago by my servant Joseph Smith, Jr. The shape and character of the building is to conform to ministries which will be carried out within its walls. These functions I will reveal through my servant the prophet and his counselors from time to time, as need for more specific direction arises.[3]

The instruction did not include building the temple at that time, which caused some misunderstanding among some members of the RLDS church.

An important understanding of the physical nature of the temple was explained in a 1970 World Conference report by the RLDS church's First Presidency. In this report they stated that the

temple is not now thought to be a single structure of monumental proportions, but...a complex which provides for a variety of functions which are appropriate to a Zionic community when they are undertaken in the spirit of worship. The Auditorium is already serving some of these purposes and can be regarded as part of the "Temple Complex." The next most urgent need is to provide facilities for a high quality program of ministerial and ledership education, including libraries, consultation and seminar rooms, and a public museum which preserves and displays and interprets the artifacts of our spiritual heritage.[4]

Additional information and confirmation was given to the RLDS church by way of revelation in April 1984:

My servants have been diligent in the work of planning for the building of my temple in the Center Place. Let this work continue at an accelerated rate, according to the instructions already given, for there is great need of the spiritual awakening that will be engendered by the ministries experienced within its walls....

The temple shall be dedicated to the pursuit of peace. It shall be for reconciliation and for healing of the spirit. It shall also be for a strengthening of faith and preparation for witness. By its ministries an attitude of wholeness of body, mind, and spirit as a desirable end toward which to strive will be fostered. It shall be the means for providing leadership education for priesthood and member. And it shall be a place in which the essential meaning of the Restoration as healing and redeeming agent is given new life and understanding, inspired by the life and witness of the Redeemer of the world.

Therefore, let the work of planning go forward, and let the resources be gathered in, that the building of my temple may be an ensign to the world of the breadth and depth of the devotion of the Saints.[5]

The work of planning is going forward on all aspects of the temple building, including the funding. RLDS members are eager for the day when they will participate in the temple ministries described in the revelation received in April 1984.

* * *

The LDS church has a very different understanding of the temple and its functions. One prominent aspect is that the LDS church believes temples should be built in as many places around the world as possible. At this writing there are more than forty of these structures being built or already in service in many parts of the world.

It is very important for members of the LDS church to live worthy lives in order to qualify for a "temple recommend"—a document issued by local ecclesiastical authorities—so that they can attend the temple to receive their own endowment, and then to continually visit the temple to receive endowments on behalf of persons who are deceased.

As was discussed in another chapter, baptisms are performed in the LDS temples on behalf of those who die without being baptized into the LDS church. In addition to this ordinance, deceased males are ordained to the Melchisedec priesthood. Deceased families are "sealed" for the eternities by proxy; living families are also "sealed" for eternity.

Interpreting a scripture in Malachi 4:5, 6, the LDS church finds authorization for the extensive genealogy work for which they have become world famous. This genealogy work is necessary before the ordinances for the deceased can be performed in the church's temples.

Behold, I will send you Elijah the prophet before the coming of the great and dreadful day of the Lord:

And he shall turn the heart of the fathers to the children, and the heart of the children to their fathers, lest I come and smite the earth with a curse.

David O. McKay, a former president and prophet of the LDS church, explained the purpose of the temple.

One of the distinguishing features of the restored Church of Jesus Christ is the eternal nature of its ordinances and ceremonies. . . . if earthly things are typical of heavenly things, in the spirit world we shall recognize our loved ones there and know them as we loved them here. . . . with the restoration of the Holy Priesthood, the Church asserts that this power [referring to Matthew 16:19 wherein it states: "And I will give unto thee the keys of the kingdom of heaven: and whatsoever thou shalt bind on earth shall be bound in heaven: and whatsoever thou shalt loose on earth shall be loosed in heaven."] was again given to chosen men, and that in the house of the Lord where the marriage ceremony is performed by those who are properly authorized to represent our Lord and Savior, Jesus Christ, the union between husband and wife, and between parents and children, is effected for time and all eternity, and that for those thus married the family will continue into the eternities. . . .

Those who accept Jesus Christ, our Lord, as the author of salvation: those who accept his statements—unqualified statements—regarding the necessity of obedience to certain principles are bound to admit that everybody must comply with certain fundamental ordinances or else nobody need comply with them. Now that is the plain fact. . . .

The words of the Savior to Nicodemus are accepted in their literal sense by faithful members of the Church. The scriptures make no distinction between the living and the dead. This law is of universal application, exemption being granted only to children who die in infancy, having no sin to expiate. To provide a means of salvation for all, facilities are made available in the temples whereby the living may be baptized in behalf of the deceased. . . .

Since the restoration of this principle and practice, church members have zealously searched the records of the world for the history of their ancestors that their forefathers might receive vicariously the blessings of the gospel of Christ. In connection with this work the church maintains an extensive genealogical organization.

These two great purposes—eternal marriage [binding the family for time and eternity], and opening the door of the kingdom for those who have died without an adequate opportunity to accept the gospel of Jesus Christ and its essential ordinances—when preached properly, earnestly, and sincerely to the honest-in-heart, will appeal to the justice of those who love the truth.

In addition there is the temple "endowment," which is also an ordinance pertaining to man's eternal journey and limitless possibilities and progress which a just and loving Father has provided for the children whom he made in his own image—for the whole human family.[6]

LDS temples are not public houses of worship, and after they have been dedicated, only those members of the church judged to be in good standing by their local ecclesiastical leaders are able to gain entrance. Although they are closed to the public, the LDS church maintains that the temple ordinances are not secret, but sacred.

The late LDS church president Spencer W. Kimball has spoken often of the temple and its importance, and the duties of the church members in relation to the work of the temple.

There is an urgency to engage more fully in the redeeming of our kindred dead through more frequent temple attendance. All those who possess temple recommends should use them as often as possible to engage in baptism, endowments, and sealings for the dead. Other members of the Church should concern themselves seriously with preparations to qualify for temple recommends that they, too, might enjoy these eternal blessings and also act as saviors on Mount Zion. There is an ever-increasing burden of temple work to be done by the Saints, and we should rise to meet this challenge.[7]

SUMMARY

1. Temples have been a prominent theme since the organization of the Latter Day Saint church in the 1830s.

2. The first temple of the Latter Day Saint movement was constructed at Kirtland, Ohio, and dedicated by Joseph Smith, Jr., in 1836.

3. The RLDS church believes temples are public houses of worship which provide ministries for the living.

4. Definite instructions pertaining to the construction of a temple came to the RLDS church by way of revelation in 1968 and again in 1984.

5. The temple is perceived by the RLDS church to be one component structure of a complex of facilities which provide for a variety of functions.

6. The RLDS temple in Independence is now in the planning and development stages, and both members and leaders of the RLDS church anticipate its construction in the near future.

7. The LDS church believes temples should be built in as many places as possible. More than forty buildings have been constructed in many parts of the world.

8. LDS church members must obtain a "temple recommend" from their local ecclesiastical leaders before they are able to gain entrance to a temple.

9. LDS temples are places where living persons can be "sealed" to each other for eternity. More especially, temples are seen as the only place where baptism, confirmation, priesthood ordination, and eternal marriages can be performed by proxy on behalf of deceased persons.

10. The LDS church, famous for its genealogy facilities and work, believes that church members must search out their ancestors and perform temple ordinances for them.

NOTES

1. Roy A. Cheville, "The Temple in Today's Church Life," *Saints' Herald* 116 (April 1969): 20.
2. *Saints' Herald* 115 (June 1, 1968): 364.
3. RLDS Doctrine and Covenants 149:6a.
4. *Conference Minutes,* 1970, pp. 240, 41.
5. RLDS Doctrine and Covenants 156:3–6.
6. David O. McKay, *The purpose of the Temple,* n.d. A pamphlet published by the LDS church, Salt Lake City.
7. Kimball, 540–541.

8

TITHING AND THE STEWARDSHIP PRINCIPLE

Tithing, and the broader principle of stewardship of which it is a part, plays a significant role in the lives of Latter Day Saint believers.

The Old Testament provides a basis for tithing and its interpretation. Scriptural record on this law goes back to the earliest times in biblical history. In the books of Moses the workings of this concept are described in detail. The most quoted scripture from the Old Testament regarding tithing, however, is found in Malachi 3:8–10: "Will a man rob God? Yet ye have robbed me. But ye say, Wherein have we robbed thee? In tithes and offerings. . . . Bring ye all the tithes into the storehouse."

Few details about tithing are provided in the early revelations to the Restoration, perhaps because church members were attempting to live what was considered the fuller law—that of consecration. Except for mention of the word, with accompanying warnings, the only section issued by Joseph Smith, Jr., contained in the Doctrine and Covenants that deals specifically with the workings of tithing is Doctrine and Covenants 106 (LDS Doctrine and Covenants 119). There is additional material in the LDS edition, much of which has not been canonized by the RLDS church, but is contained in the church histories. This relatively short revelation was given in 1838 in response to Joseph's inquiry on the subject:

Verily, thus saith the Lord, I require all their surplus property to be put into the hands of the bishop of my church of Zion, for the building of mine house, and for the laying the foundation of

Zion, and for the priesthood, and for the debts of the presidency of my church; and this shall be the beginning of the tithing of my people; and after that, those who have thus been tithed, shall pay one tenth of all their interest annually; and this shall be a standing law unto them forever, for my holy priesthood, saith the Lord.[1]

Over the years the RLDS and LDS interpretations of tithing have developed quite differently, particularly in the interpretation of what is meant by the word *interest*.

In the days of Joseph Smith, Jr., this concept was defined to mean that part of a person's income left after family needs were met. This was explained in a treatise written by Apostle Orson Hyde (who followed Brigham Young to Utah) which was published in an official publication of the church.

The celestial law requires one-tenth part of all a man's substance which he possesses at the time he comes into the church, and one-tenth part of his annual increase ever after. If it requires all a man can earn to support himself and his family, he is not tithed at all. The celestial law does not take the mother's and children's bread, neither ought else which they really need for comfort. The poor that have not this world's goods to spare, but serve and honor God according to the best of their abilities in every other way, shall have a celestial crown in the Eternal Kingdom of our Father.[2]

One of the most important concepts related to tithing is the principle of accountability. This idea is connected with that of agency, wherein a person is permitted to act for oneself, but with the responsibility to choose between life or death, good or evil.

Because God grants persons their agency, they become accountable for their stewardship over life. The belief of the church is that each person must make an accounting to God in this life through his authorized servants, as well as at the Day of Judgment.[3]

In practical operation, RLDS church members donate one-tenth of their increase to the church. Increase is that portion of the annual income that is not spent for basic living needs such as food, clothing, and shelter. This tithing money is managed by the Presiding Bishopric, and used to finance the operations of the church.

At the end of each year, members are asked to complete and submit to the Presiding Bishop an Annual Stewardship Accounting or Tithing Statement.

This financial accounting is not merely a financial report of one person to another; it is an accounting to God through his church. The tithing statement is first a tangible expression of one's willingness to acknowledge personal stewardship under God's ownership; second, a methodical way to determine the tithe accurately; third, a way of keeping one's self informed of the use being made of financial resources and opportunities; and fourth, an acknowledgment of one's unity with the church in a cooperative endeavor with other persons and God to "establish the cause of Zion."

The presenting of the tithing statement to the Presiding Bishop is voluntary and is a significant act of worship.[4]

The stewardship concept encompasses not only tithing, but a much broader understanding of our relationship with God. This has been explained in a revelation to the RLDS church in 1964, and is found in the Doctrine and Covenants 147:5 (since this section was given through the RLDS prophet, it is not found in the LDS edition of the Doctrine and Covenants):

Stewardship is the response of my people to the ministry of my Son and is required alike of all those who seek to build the kingdom.... Repression of unnecessary wants is in harmony with the law of stewardship and becomes my people.

The basic principles of stewardship, and its importance to the members of the RLDS church, have been explained:

Four principles have emerged in our thinking as specific expressions of the overall concept of stewardship. These have been thought of primarily in financial terms but apply equally to all of our resources. First is inheritance. This applies to all of the resources that are ours when we are born into the world and those that are given at subsequent times in our lives. Inheritance applies to that which is ours to manage and use as stewards under God. Like the servants in Jesus' parable of the talents, we do not all receive the same things in like quantities. Yet our calling is the same: to use what we have for the enrichment of our own lives and the lives of others. We need to recognize all of the various aspects of our inheritances and the potential uses they have. In this way we can respond to stewardship in the most effective way.

The second principle is increase. As we use our resources a primary concern is providing for our own existence and growth. We realize, however, that most of us are blessed with more than the basic needs of life and that many other people in the world go wanting. Frequently we enjoy luxuries while some people die from lack of food and shelter. It is appropriate, therefore, that we abstain from consuming all our resources ourselves in order to share our productivity in meaningful ways with others. Increase results when stewards adopt a lifestyle in which they intentionally have financial resources, time, and abilities beyond what they consider to be their basic needs.

The accumulation of increase is important for providing long-term security for ourselves. Investment in a house or in education, for example, and the accumulation of savings, are uses of increase that recognize the importance of providing for future needs. Increase—through tithes, offerings, and oblation—is also used for the support of the work of the church, as well as to benefit others who may be in need.

The third principle of stewardship, surplus, is a method for making our increase available for the use of others. After we have made provision for what we estimate to be our needs, we can make our surplus resources available for others to use.

These surplus resources are consecrated for specific ministries through a storehouse which is the fourth stewardship principle. In some jurisdictions of the church, particularly some stakes, the storehouse principle takes the form of actual accumulations of money and material goods which are available for distribution to those who need these things. Such is not the case in many places, however, and cannot be when the principle is applied to surpluses of time, skills and other intangibles. Yet the lack of storehouses of actual goods does not mean an absence of the principle at work. Some of the most effective expressions of the storehouse principle are found in the sharing of various intangible resources. Too frequently we overlook our surpluses of skills and other intangibles and unintentionally withhold their availability from the church and from others.[5]

Stewardship, then, is the concept of which tithing is a part, and continues to play a prominent role in the lives of RLDS church members.

The LDS church has not emphasized stewardship in modern-day practice, but teaches the payment of one's tithing, and contribution to welfare and other church funds which have been established for caring for those in need. A prominent church leader has written the following:

Under the law of consecration, as it operated through the United Order, church members consecrated, conveyed, and deeded all their property to the Lord's agent. Then they received back to use in supporting their own family a stewardship....underlying this principle of stewardship is the eternal gospel truth that all things belong to the Lord....it is by the wise use of one's stewardship that eternal life is won.[6]

In the LDS church tithing is considered one of the most important commandments to be obeyed by the individual member. Before a person can be ordained to a priesthood office, his presiding officer must ascertain whether the candidate is a full tithe payer. In addition, priesthood leaders and members are told that "an ultimate goal...is to inspire...the...family, to conform to all Church standards, including...payment of tithing."[7]

The late LDS apostle LeGrand Richards explained that

first, tithing is the most equitable manner of financing [God's] church, for the burden is distributed according to one's ability to pay....Second, tithing was instituted to test the faith of his people, obedience to the law of tithing being accompanied by a promised blessing. Hence, it [tithing] is the Lord's law of blessing his people.[8]

The LDS church has interpreted "increase" to mean a person's gross income, before needs such as food, clothing, or shelter are taken care of. For church members to be considered worthy to enter the temples of the church, they must be full tithing payers.

Each year during the last few days of December, church members are to meet with their bishop and with him go over their personal contribution records for the year. This is known as "tithing settlement."[9]

The late LDS president Spencer W. Kimball has stated that he believes tithing to be a solution for poverty—that the poor have a special need to tithe:

There are people who say they cannot afford to pay tithing, because their incomes are small. They are the people who need the blessings of the Lord! No one is ever too poor to pay tithing, and the Lord has promised that he will open the windows of heaven when we are obedient to his law. He can give us better salaries, he can give us more judgment in the spending of our money. He can give us better health, he can give us greater understanding so that we can get better positions. He can help us so that we can do all the things we want to do. However, if we like luxuries or even necessities more than we like obedience, we will miss the blessings which he would like to give us.[10]

SUMMARY

1. Tithing is only one part of the broader principle of stewardship.

2. The law of tithing goes back to the earliest of times in biblical history.

3. Tithing, as practiced in both the RLDS and LDS churches today, was formalized in 1838.

4. In RLDS practice, tithing means 10 percent of one's increase—that portion remaining after one has provided for the basic needs of life.

5. Four concepts are understood by RLDS church members as related to stewardship: inheritance, increase, surplus, and storehouse.

6. In LDS practice, tithing means 10 percent of one's increase—interpreted to mean gross earnings, before any deductions are allowed.

7. In LDS belief, tithing is a strict commandment, full observance of which is required to be a member in good standing.

NOTES

1. RLDS Doctrine and Covenants 106:1; LDS Doctrine and Covenants 119:1.
2. The *Millennial Star*, Vol. 9, p. 12.
3. *The Priesthood Manual*, 287–88.
4. Ibid.
5. Judd and Cole, 141–42.
6. McConkie, 766–67.
7. *Melchizedek Priesthood Handbook*, 1975, pp. 11, 20.
8. Richards, 367.
9. McConkie, 799.
10. Kimball, 212–13.

9

ZION

Those familiar with the Jewish faith might believe they understand the meaning of *Zion*. Indeed, many parallels can be drawn between the Jewish belief and the Latter Day Saint belief. Zion is an important facet of the Latter Day Saint way of life and has been so from the earliest years of the Restoration movement.

One of the first recorded statements concerning Zion is found in Section 6 of the Doctrine and Covenants. This revelation was recorded in April 1829 and was addressed to Oliver Cowdery. In this document Cowdery is admonished, among other things, to "seek to bring forth and establish the cause of Zion."

Since that time there have been numerous references to Zion in the recorded revelatory documents brought to the church by the prophets.

One of the most important of these documents was given in 1831 while Joseph Smith and other church leaders were in Jackson County, Missouri, attempting to establish a community of church members. Section 57 in the Doctrine and Covenants, given in July 1831, is the first document that specifically gives the location of the place where Zion was to be established. Joseph Smith, Jr., wrote:

This [Jackson County, Missouri] is the land of promise, and the place for the city of Zion.... The place which is now called Independence, is the Center Place, and the spot for the temple is lying westward upon a lot which is not far from the courthouse.

And so Zion has been established, at least in the minds of the Latter Day Saints, as a real place waiting to be built.

Over the years the RLDS church has earnestly sought to interpret the concept of Zion into terms that church members both in the United States as well as in other lands could relate to. Writing in 1970, the Basic Beliefs Committee stated the following:

We believe that Zion is the means by which the prophetic church participates in the world to embody the divine intent for all personal and social relations. Zion is the implementation of those principles, processes, and relationships which give concrete expression to the power of the kingdom of God in the world. It affirms the concern of the gospel with the structures of our common life together and promotes the expression of God's reconciling love in the world, thus bringing forth the divine life in human society. The church is called to gather her covenant people into signal communities where they live out the will of God in the total life of society. While this concrete expression of the kingdom of God must have a central point of beginning it reaches out to every part of the world where the prophetic church is in mission.[1]

This idea of Zion is closely related to the concept of the kingdom of God. Early church members saw these two as one and the same, and in their millennial zeal sought to prepare themselves and a place to receive the literal establishment of God's kingdom and the return of Jesus Christ.

The idea of a perfect society living in peace and righteousness is not unique to the Latter Day Saints. Many people throughout the history of the world have attempted to establish Zion-like communities.

Although still understood by many to be a literal place yet to be built, Zion is also seen by the RLDS church as a process, a condition, and a people.

This understanding of Zion is seen as the fulfillment of the prophecy recorded by both Isaiah and Micah, and it is through this idea that the church attempts to relate to prevailing societal conditions in the world to bring about these ideals:

And it shall come to pass in the last days, when the mountain of the Lord's house shall be established in the top of the mountains, and shall be exalted above the hills, and all nations shall flow unto it. And many people shall go and say, Come ye, and let us go up the mountain of the Lord, to the house of the God of Jacob; and he will teach us of his ways, and we will walk in his paths; for out of Zion shall go forth the law, and the word of the Lord from Jerusalem.[2]

The early Latter Day Saints operated under the concept that Zion was a literal place they would build and be gathered in various communities where they could live their beliefs. They attempted to build cities composed not only of church-related establishments, but also businesses and educational organizations—complete communities based on religion but also including all other aspects of everyday life.

Because of the designation of Independence, Missouri, as the Center Place, some RLDS church members believe that a Zionic community can be located only in that place. Other church members believe, however, that Zionic communities can be established in many other areas throughout the world. The stake organization of the church, which is organized in those areas with higher concentrations of members, has helped members more fully understand this viewpoint. Church writers have expressed this idea:

Related to this question of the location of Zion as a place is the whole matter of whether Zion is more appropriately seen as a remnant gathered to a specific location or as the leaven enriching all of society. It would appear that if Zion is seen as a remnant gathered to just one place (Independence, Missouri) then it is exclusive. This is unfortunate because Zion, even if understood as a remnant or special group of people, is after all not just for our benefit. It shines as a light on a hill assisting the world to come to Christ. Zion, as the gathered of the Lord, may exist in a number of places rather than just one. Thus, the impact on the world is measurably increased. The implementation of

Zionic principles in one culture or place will be different from other Zionic communities.

Zion as leaven ought to exist wherever we live. For some, however, such a concept of Zion produces fear that it will become diluted and not identifiable anyplace. For many, on the other hand, it means being on the forefront of living discipleship. The concept of Zion as leaven keeps before us the overall goal to which Zionic endeavors are directed: the redemption of the entire world.

We can therefore conclude that both remnant and leaven images can help us in identifying the nature and the call to establish Zion in our day. Yet both images also have the danger of obscuring the real intent of this call. The important point is that even though we are specifically called by God to establish Zion, we are called to do this on behalf of God for the benefit of the whole world and not just for our own enrichment.[3]

In discussing the important aspects of Zion—that of Zion as a process and a condition, a missionary tract published by the RLDS church proclaims that Zion as a process

is affirmed in the Bible when Christ is quoted as teaching his disciples: "The kingdom of God cometh not by observation: Neither shall they say, Lo, here! or, lo there! for, behold, the kingdom of God is within [or, in the midst of] you."—Luke 17:20, 21[4]

The concept of Zion, sounded in the Old Testament and taught by Christ, has been in the process of growing for centuries. The Church of Jesus Christ is called to continue the process of relating the Zionic ideal to today's society. It is a non-ending task. Societies and cultures are always in need of transformation to remove the causes of suffering, dehumanization, and injustice. As new problems and structures arise, new answers and processes are needed. Human society means continued change and a lack of final answers. Zion is a process always rising to meet the need.

Israel A. Smith, president of the RLDS church in

1947, told the Saints, "Zionic conditions are no further away nor any closer than the spiritual condition of my people justifies." Zion is a process marked and recognizable only by the spiritual condition of the people. It is an attitude and a way of life. In the Doctrine and Covenants is stated, "Let Zion rejoice, for this is Zion, the pure in heart" (94:5c; LDS 97:21).

The principle of stewardship is seen as being very basic to the establishment of Zion, as explained by the Basic Beliefs Committee:

Traditionally, the Reorganized Church of Jesus Christ of Latter Day Saints has believed that all are called to be stewards under God. This means that discipleship involves one's total life and the use of all his powers and resources in service to God. This is more than individual stewardship; it is social responsibility. The church as a corporate, integrated community in which the members are joined together in one body reveals the meaning of the incarnation as it is lived out by that body in the affairs of life. Because of this fact, the church in the early days of its existence often found itself in conflict with those denominations that stressed salvation by faith. Salvation by faith was interpreted by many to mean that salvation is guaranteed when one accepts Christ through giving some outward confession of belief in him. Such salvation, however, was interpreted in terms of a life after death in which one escaped eternal punishment and entered into the joys of heaven. Latter Day Saints insisted that religion involved the totality of life and, therefore, they stressed the necessity of works....

It is important to affirm that there are no divisions between the secular and the divine. The activities of business, politics, education, etc., are not separate from the realms of religion. Indeed, it is our faith that all of life is of concern to God and through the Zionic community the church may live out the will of God in all personal and social relations as well as in its ecclesiastical functions.[5]

* * *

Many of the concepts regarding Zion as understood by RLDS church members, would probably find place in the faith of many members of the LDS church. Certainly, the historical perspective of Zion as a place in the early history of the Restoration would be commonly related as historical fact. Then too, both churches have the writings of Joseph Smith, Jr., and others involved in the early church, to help modern-day members understand what those first members were thinking and teaching about Zion.

One prominent LDS theologian has composed seven different meanings for the word *Zion*.

1. Zion is the name given by the Lord to his saints; it is the name by which the Lord's people are always identified. . . . Thus The Church of Jesus Christ of Latter-day Saints is Zion. Joining the Church is becoming a citizen of Zion. . . .

2. After the Lord had called his people Zion, Enoch "built a city that was called the City of Holiness, even Zion. . . ."

3. At least from the days of King David, the name Zion was applied to one of the hills upon which Jerusalem is built or (later) to the entire city. Solomon built his temple in Zion.

4. The New Jerusalem to be built in Jackson County, Missouri, is also called the City of Zion or Zion. . . .

5. Joseph Smith announced at the April, 1844, general conference of the church that all of North and South America comprise the land of Zion. . . .

6. At the Second Coming, "The Lamb shall stand upon Mount Zion, and with him a hundred and forty-four thousand, having his Father's name written on their foreheads." [LDS Doctrine and Covenants 133:18, Revelation 14:1–5.] The Mount Zion spoken of is identified by latter-day revelation as the New Jerusalem to be built in Jackson County, Missouri. [LDS Doctrine and Covenants 84:1–4, RLDS 83.]

7. Paul uses the term Mount Zion to refer to the abode of exalted beings, those who overcome all things and inherit the fulness of the Father's kingdom.[6]

Closely associated with the LDS understanding of Zion, is the belief in the gathering of Israel and the return of the ten lost tribes. The LDS church's "Tenth Article of Faith" states the following:

> We believe in the literal gathering of Israel and in the restoration of the Ten Tribes; that Zion (the New Jerusalem) will be built upon the American continent; that Christ will reign personally upon the earth; and, that the earth will be renewed and receive its paradisiacal glory.[7]

Although in the early history of the LDS church, members were encouraged to gather to Utah, the current teaching is to encourage church members to remain in their native lands, where stakes have been established. Just as the RLDS church believes that the stake organization of the church is an extension of Zion, so also does the LDS church believe regarding this organizational unit.

The late LDS church president Spencer W. Kimball has written that there are

> three fundamental things we must do if we are to "bring again Zion," three things for which we who labor for Zion must commit ourselves.
>
> First, we must eliminate the individual tendency to selfishness that snares the soul, shrinks the heart, and darkens the mind. . . .
>
> It is incumbent upon us to put away selfishness in our families, our business and professional pursuits, and our Church affairs. . . .
>
> Second, we must cooperate completely and work in harmony one with the other. There must be unanimity in our decisions and unity in our actions. . . .
>
> If the Spirit of the Lord is to magnify our labors, then this spirit of oneness and cooperation must be the prevailing spirit in all that we do. . . .
>
> Third, we must lay on the altar and sacrifice whatever is required by the Lord. We begin by offering a "broken heart and a contrite spirit." We follow this by giving our best effort in our assigned fields of labor and callings. We learn our duty and execute it fully. Finally we consecrate our time, talents, and means as called upon by our file leaders and as prompted by the whisperings of the Spirit. In the church . . . we can give expres-

sion to every ability, every righteous desire, every thoughtful impulse.[8]

A visitor to the South Visitors Center on LDS Temple Square in Salt Lake City, Utah, is met with the prophecy of Isaiah (as quoted above) in large letters on the wall. Many LDS have taken this prophecy to mean that God moved Zion from Missouri to Utah, and that Utah, being in the mountains, is specifically what is meant by the "mountain of the Lord's house" (or the LDS temple) being established "in the tops of the mountains." The late LDS apostle Bruce R. McConkie has explained this seeming contradiction:

This great prophecy, as is often the case, is subject to the law of multiple fulfillment. 1. In Salt Lake City and other mountain locations temples, in the full and true sense of the word, have been erected, and representatives of all nations are flowing unto them to learn of God and his ways. In this connection and as part of the general fulfillment of Isaiah's prophecy, is the fact that one of the world's greatest genealogical societies has been established in Salt Lake City—a society to which people of all nations come to do the ancestral research which must precede the performance of vicarious temple ordinances. 2. But the day is yet future when the Lord's house is to be built on that "Mount Zion" which is "the city of New Jerusalem" in Jackson County, Missouri. Mount Zion, itself, will be the mountain of the Lord's house in the day when that glorious temple is erected. 3. When the Jews flee unto Jerusalem, it will be "unto the mountains of the Lord's house," for a holy temple is to be built there also as part of the work of the great era of restoration.

The law cannot go forth from Zion and the word of the Lord from Jerusalem, in the full millennial sense that Isaiah foresaw and specified, until these two great future temples are constructed in the old and new Jerusalems.[9]

LDS church members believe that the New Jerusalem spoken of above will be built by them at some future date, not yet revealed. This New Jerusalem will be built by church members, and also will come down from heaven, with the two parts of the city uniting as one.[10]

Associated with this concept is that of the kingdom of God. Church members believe that the LDS church, as presently constituted, is the literal kingdom of God on earth, and that nothing more needs to be done to establish this kingdom.

It is believed that during the millennium this kingdom will continue on earth, but will be at that time both a religious and a political kingdom. Then the LDS church believes it will have the rule and government of the world given to it.[11]

SUMMARY

1. The concept of Zion was established early in the history of the Restoration churches.

2. Early church members understood Zion more as a literal place they were to build than as a process or a condition.

3. The RLDS church places emphasis on the creation of a Zionic society in all parts of the world, while maintaining a belief that Jackson County, Missouri, is the Center Place.

4. The idea of the kingdom of God and the idea of Zion are closely related in the RLDS perception.

5. Zion and the related conditions are directly connected with the spirituality of church members in the RLDS understanding.

6. The Latter Day Saint concept of Zion is seen by both the RLDS and LDS churches as a fulfillment of the prophecy of Isaiah.

7. The LDS church believes that Salt Lake City, its headquarters, is Zion and has partially fulfilled Isaiah's prophecy.

8. Sometime in the future, according to LDS beliefs, Zion and the city of New Jerusalem will be established in Jackson County, Missouri.

9. The return of the ten lost tribes of Israel is a significant factor in the LDS beliefs about Zion.

10. LDS church membership automatically grants a person Zionic citizenship.

NOTES

1. *Exploring the Faith*, 172.
2. Isaiah 2:2–3; Micah 4:1–2.
3. Judd and Cole, 130.
4. *What Is Zion?* (Independence, Missouri: Herald Publishing House, n.d.), 5–6.
5. *Exploring the Faith*, 175–76.
6. McConkie, 854–55.
7. *Pearl of Great Price*, 61.
8. Kimball, 363–64.
9. McConkie, 518.
10. Ibid., 532.
11. Ibid., 416.

APPENDIX

Book of Mormon and Doctrine and Covenants Cross Reference

RLDS	LDS	RLDS	LDS	RLDS	LDS
FIRST BOOK OF NEPHI		**Second Nephi continued**		**Mosiah continued**	
Chapter	Chapter	Chapter	Chapter	Chapter	Chapter
1:1	1:1	9:61	19:1	1:92	3:1
1:24	2:1	9:82	20:1	2:1	4:1
1:59	3:1	9:116	21:1	3:1	5:1
1:99	4:1	9:132	22:1	4:1	6:1
1:146	5:1	10:1	23:1	5:1	7:1
2:1	6:1	10:23	24:1	5:53	8:1
2:7	7:1	11:1	25:1	6:1	9:1
2:40	8:1	11:58	26:1	6:26	10:1
2:92	9:1	11:116	27:1	7:1	11:1
3:1	10:1	12:1	28:1	7:45	12:1
3:37	11:1	12:42	29:1	7:100	13:1
3:96	12:1	12:75	30:1	8:1	13:25
3:135	13:1	13:1	31:1	8:15	14:1
3:201	14:1	14:1	32:1	8:28	15:1
4:1	15:1	15:1	33:1	8:70	16:1
5:1	16:1			9:1	17:1
5:55	17:1	**BOOK OF JACOB**		9:28	18:1
5:168	18:1	1:1	1:1	9:74	19:1
5:218	19:1	2:1	2:1	9:108	20:1
6:1	19:22	2:48	3:1	9:140	21:1
6:8	20:1	3:1	4:1	10:1	22:1
6:30	21:1	3:30	5:1	11:1	23:1
7:1	22:1	4:1	6:1	11:44	24:1
		5:1	7:1	11:77	25:1
				11:105	26:1
SECOND BOOK OF NEPHI		**BOOK OF ENOS**		11:150	27:1
1:1	1:1	1:1	1:1	12:1	28:1
1:59	2:1			13:1	28:20
2:1	3:1			13:3	29:1
3:1	4:1	**BOOK OF JAROM**			
4:1	5:1	1:1	1:1		
5:1	6:1			**BOOK OF ALMA**	
5:46	7:1			1:1	1:1
5:70	8:1	**BOOK OF OMNI**		1:53	2:1
6:1	9:1	1:1	1:1	1:98	3:1
7:1	10:1			2:1	4:1
8:1	11:1			3:1	5:1
8:17	12:1	**WORDS OF MORMON**		4:1	6:1
8:39	13:1	1:1	1:1	5:1	7:1
8:65	14:1			6:1	8:1
8:71	15:1			7:1	9:1
9:1	16:1	**BOOK OF MOSIAH**		8:1	10:1
9:14	17:1	1:1	1:1	8:48	11:1
9:39	18:1	1:28	2:1	9:1	12:1

Alma continued

RLDS Chapter	LDS Chapter
9:62	13:1
10:1	13:10
10:32	14:1
10:86	15:1
11:1	16:1
12:1	17:1
12:62	18:1
12:126	19:1
12:181	20:1
13:1	21:1
13:30	22:1
14:1	23:1
14:21	24:1
14:59	25:1
14:79	26:1
15:1	27:1
15:36	28:1
15:52	29:1
16:1	30:1
16:78	31:1
16:121	32:1
16:174	33:1
16:201	34:1
16:240	35:1
17:1	36:1
17:31	37:1
18:1	38:1
19:1	39:1
19:28	40:1
19:62	41:1
19:81	42:1
20:1	43:1
20:61	44:1
21:1	45:1
21:29	46:1
21:78	47:1
21:123	48:1
21:149	49:1
22:1	50:1
23:1	51:1
24:1	52:1
24:50	53:1
25:1	54:1
25:27	55:1
26:1	56:1
26:70	57:1
26:118	58:1
27:1	59:1
27:14	60:1
28:1	61:1
29:1	62:1
30:1	63:1

BOOK OF HELAMAN

RLDS Chapter	LDS Chapter
1:1	1:1
1:37	2:1
2:1	3:1
2:35	4:1
2:63	5:1
2:118	6:1
3:1	7:1
3:32	8:1
3:67	9:1
3:112	10:1
4:1	11:1
4:48	12:1
5:1	13:1
5:54	14:1
5:87	15:1
5:109	16:1

THIRD BOOK OF NEPHI

RLDS Chapter	LDS Chapter
1:1	1:1
1:38	2:1
2:1	3:1
2:39	4:1
2:82	5:1
3:1	6:1
3:36	7:1
4:1	8:1
4:26	9:1
4:53	10:1
5:1	11:1
5:44	12:1
5:93	13:1
6:1	13:25
6:13	14:1
7:1	15:1
7:24	16:1
8:1	17:1
8:28	18:1
9:1	19:1
9:37	20:1
9:86	21:1
10:1	21:22
10:8	22:1
10:26	23:1
11:1	23:4
11:2	24:1
11:22	25:1
11:28	26:1
12:1	26:6
12:14	27:1
13:1	27:23
13:12	28:1

Third Nephi continued

RLDS Chapter	LDS Chapter
13:54	29:1
14:1	30:1

FOURTH BOOK OF NEPHI

RLDS Chapter	LDS Chapter
1:1	1:1

BOOK OF MORMON

RLDS Chapter	LDS Chapter
1:1	1:1
1:21	2:1
1:63	3:1
2:1	4:1
2:26	5:1
3:1	6:1
3:24	7:1
4:1	8:1
4:57	9:1

BOOK OF ETHER

RLDS Chapter	LDS Chapter
1:1	1:1
1:22	2:1
1:60	3:1
1:94	4:1
2:1	5:1
3:1	6:1
3:37	7:1
3:67	8:1
4:1	9:1
4:43	10:1
4:90	11:1
5:1	12:1
6:1	13:1
6:35	14:1
6:72	15:1

BOOK OF MORONI

RLDS Chapter	LDS Chapter
1:1	1:1
2:1	2:1
3:1	3:1
4:1	4:1
5:1	5:1
6:1	6:1
7:1	7:1
8:1	8:1
9:1	9:1
10:1	10:1

DOCTRINE AND COVENANTS CROSS REFERENCE

I. These sections are numbered identically in both the LDS (Mormon) and RLDS editions:

1, 4–9, 37–76.

II. The following sections are numbered differently:

RLDS	LDS
2	3
3	10
10	11
11	12
12	14
13	15
14	16
15	17
16	18
17	20
18	19
19	21
20	22
21	23
22	24
23	24
24	25
25	26
26	27
27	28
28	29
29	30
30	31
31	32
32	33
33	34

RLDS Continued	LDS
34	35
35	36
77	78
78	79
79	80
80	81
81	82
82	83
83	84
84	86
85	88
86	89
87	90
88	91
89	92
90	93
91	94
92	95
93	96
94	97
95	98
96	99
97	100
98	101
99	102
100	103
101	104
102	105
103	106
104	107
105	112
106	119
107	124
108	133
109	127
110	128
112	134
113	135

III. The following appear in the Mormon edition, but not the RLDS edition:

★2, ★13, 77, ★★85, ★87, ★108, ★109, ★110, 111, ★113, 114, ★115, ★116, ★★117, ★118, 120, 121, 122, 123, 125, 126, 129, 130, 131, 132, 136, ★137, 138, Official Declaration 1, Official Declaration 2.

★ Appear in RLDS Church history.

★★Partially published or referred to in RLDS *Church History.*

IV. The following sections appear in the RLDS edition, but not the Mormon edition:

22, 36 (appear in Mormon Pearl of Great Price)

108A—minutes of the August 17, 1835 General Assembly of the Church.

111—section on marriage adopted by the church in 1835.

114 to 156 (as of 1984). These are revelations and instructions received through Joseph Smith III and his successors in the Presidency of the RLDS church.